YOU WERE

BORN

for

GREATNESS

Spiritual Guidance from the Angelic Realm

JACOB GLASS

ISBN-10: 149927694X
ISBN-13: 978-1499276947

DEDICATION

Also by Jacob Glass

Invocations: Calling Forth the Light That Heals
The Crabby Angels Chronicles
Starve a Bully, Feed a Champion

Epigraph

*"Is it a sacrifice to leave littleness behind, and wander not in vain?
It is not sacrifice to wake to glory. But it is sacrifice to accept
anything less than glory . . . Before the greatness that lives in you,
your poor appreciation of yourself and all the little offerings you give
slip into nothingness."* – A Course in Miracles

Table of Contents

You Were Born for Greatness

Acknowledgments

I want to take this opportunity to thank the Religious Science Churches/Spiritual Centers, Unity Churches and the Miracle Distribution Center for inviting and allowing me to come and do my thing with them. A huge thank you to all those who write me with encouraging words about my books and blogs – you keep me joyfully writing and I am happy to be a part of your spiritual path.

The generous tithes and donations of my readers and listeners have helped to establish this wonderful Joy Academy which has grown and grown for over 25 years now. The best is yet to come and I am so grateful and humbled by your wonderful generosity and kindness.

Introduction

This book is a continuation of my previous two books of daily guidance from my Spirit Guide Angels. It is my intention that it soothe and uplift you as it has me and those who read it while in blog form. Take what works for you and leave the rest. I have done my best to bring it through with an open heart and mind.

I call these three books "plop books" because the reader can simply open the book to any page or entry for a spiritual nugget or some guidance. It is not necessary to read from beginning to end, though study groups have formed around these books and many of them tend to do it that way. Do whatever feels right for you.

These books are self-published so please forgive any errors you find along the way. Try to focus more on the spirit of the content than on the exact grammatical form. I'm learning as I go.

Jacob Glass

1. *Life is Good*

"And God saw the light, that it was good . . . And God called the dry land Earth . . . and God saw that it was good . . . And the earth brought forth grass . . . and God saw that it was good . . . And God created whales, and every living creature that moveth . . . and God saw that it was good . . . and God made the beasts of the earth after his kind . . . and God saw that it was good . . . and God saw every thing that he had made, and, behold, it was very good." -Genesis, chapter 1

LIFE IS GOOD. God is good. You are good. People are good. The world is good. And more than that, life is meant to be enjoyed and you are meant to be happy. You were not sent to Earth to suffer, nor to be tested and tried. You CHOSE to come here in order to joyfully create and grow.

We fully understand what a radical teaching this is and that We may have lost a lot of our readers right there. Many of you have become so accustomed to thinking of the world as anything but good – of thinking of yourselves as anything but good – and certainly of thinking of humans in general as anything but good. You are much more comfortable with the idea that life is a struggle, a place of loss and pain interrupted by fleeting moments or episodes of peace and joy. Some misunderstood spiritual systems have even led you to believe that *"life is suffering."* And it is true - that *is* the world that many of YOU have made in your own minds, and since projection makes perception, you will SEE the world that you believe in. We are here to Help you to turn that all around – to build a NEW foundation.

Begin right there with the thought that life is good, God is good, the world is good, you are good and people are good. When We say all these things, We mean that their essential nature is good. Of course We see that there is violence, destruction, rage, suffering and all manner of horrible things happening upon the earth at any given moment of the day or night. But this is not because of an error in the nature of anyone or anything – it is because so many have forgotten Who and What they are. You have lost your sense of steady connection to Source, to Life Itself. You tend to lose your awareness of Essence as you get caught up in the story, story, story of the *"serial adventures of the body"* on Earth. That story is NOT Who or What you are.

Understand that when We say "good" We are speaking to you from the Absolute. Language cannot truly describe anything that is truly real in an accurate and totally satisfying way, but We must make the attempt. We are not speaking of good as opposed to "bad" – when We speak of Light, We are not speaking of the opposite of "dark." These are the assumptions humans tend to make from the vantage point of the world of pairs of opposites. In Reality, there is only ONEness. There is not even unity, for that implies opposites joining. The more you can embrace the concept of the ONE, the easier it will be for you to make the transition to truly understanding the goodness that is the ESSENCE of all Life, including your wonderful self.

And so We begin here, because this is the foundation on which everything We want to share with you will be built. We have started with perhaps the most radical teaching possible for humans to grasp because We know that you are ready, are you not? If you are, let your heart and soul say "Yes!" and off We go!

2. You Were Born for Greatness

"Is it a sacrifice to leave littleness behind, and wander not in vain? It is not sacrifice to wake to glory. But it is sacrifice to accept anything less than glory . . . Before the greatness that lives in you, your poor appreciation of yourself and all the little offerings you give slip into nothingness." -A Course in Miracles

YOU ARE A CHILD OF THE COSMOS, created from stardust as an extension of the One Life. There is nothing you need to do to achieve your inherent greatness. Nothing you have ever done, no mistake you have ever made, has diminished the Light that you are - nor has it changed your true nature.

This greatness is nothing you need to step into or claim. Do not add stress and resistance by thinking of this as something to aspire to. In fact, the process is one of awakening to what already has been achieved from the very beginning. You did not make yourself. You are not becoming great, you are simply accepting this greatness as already accomplished. On that end, there is no doing at all.

Your most important "doing" will be a process of gently undoing and letting go of all the thought forms that tempt you to believe in your littleness. The voice within that tells you that you are not good enough, that you are limited, that you cannot be or do or have a life of joy and successful living is the littleness that must be gently dissolved and neutralized each time it arises. There is nothing to fear – nothing to do battle against. Littleness is nothing more than an old mental habit pattern that can be reversed. There is no enemy trying to stop you. Even "ego" is a fictional character with no reality whatsoever. We merely use it as a word to describe a thought system that is rooted in fear and limitation.

As you begin to dissolve each habitual thought of littleness, all that will be left is your essential greatness. It is already ever-present - merely covered over by the rubble of lies and distortions that tell you that you are somehow separate from the Whole. Part of you already knows that this is True. We are speaking to that part of you now. Listen and believe. Feel this Truth awakening the Wisdom in your cells as it effortlessly dissolves all fear, guilt, shame and resistance. Allow the Truth to wash away all littleness, grievances and resentments as it melts away blockages, stress and dis-ease. Let each breath bathe you in the Golden Light of Cosmic Grace – and allow the process to be easy and pleasurable.

What want to take you on a happy journey, starting today - a journey in recognizing Who you are. For at least the next 30 days We suggest that you begin each day by looking in the mirror, gazing into your own eyes and saying aloud, *"I was born for greatness, and I am made from stardust. I am part of the Infinite Cosmos and my world is lit by miracles today."* Do not rush this. Breathe it in and accept it for yourself. There is no effort in this. You are not trying to make something be true – it already is true. There is no need to MAKE the sky be blue - the clouds have only temporarily obscured it. This is process we are now undertaking – the gentle removal of the littleness that temporarily blocks the view of your essential greatness.

Remind yourself frequently throughout the day,

"Nothing is hindering me. I was born for greatness and miracles are lighting my path with joyful ease today."

3. Coast More

"When peace comes at last to those who wrestle with temptation and fight against the giving in to sin; when the light comes at last into the mind given to contemplation; or when the goal is finally achieved by anyone, it is always with just one happy realization; "I need do nothing."" -A Course in Miracles

IF YOU COULD <u>DO</u> YOUR WAY TO ENLIGHTENMENT and inner peace, you would have been there a long time ago. The path of least resistance is the one path that frightens Westerners the most and this is why even your "spiritual" practices tend to be so aggressive and even stressful. This torment is self-inflicted and quite often worn as a badge of honor. Multi-tasking is nothing to be proud of for it tends to activate resistance within. This resistance causes tremendous friction to the body's moving parts both inner and outer – and friction wears down these parts.

You have no idea how easily all could be accomplished by savoring and enjoying more and struggling less. The endless ambition to accomplish and achieve, to check things off your "to do" list, to fight off aging and disease – all of these are costing you your peace, your joy, and your health of body and mind. Many of you are ferociously paddling a sailboat against the wind. Too often you want what doesn't want you and you are going after what will only bring you more problems and stress.

What if you simply decided to begin walking through the open doors instead of banging your head against the ones that are locked? What if you decided to stop all the furious pedaling uphill and began coasting downhill more? What if you let go of focusing on endless "improvements" and focused on savoring and enjoying? What if instead of trying to change the physical, you decided to simply change your mind ABOUT the physical? What if you stopped trying to MAKE things work, stepped back and ALLOWED everything to adjust itself while you simply flowed positive energy into your world? What if instead of anxiously trying to find the pathway, you allowed the path to find you?

Right here, right now, all things are held perfectly in the hands of God. And this does not mean that you will just sit around all day bored waiting for your eventual bankruptcy and homelessness to arrive - quite the opposite. When you release stressful motivation, what is born is a joyous inspiration. As you begin to follow your joy you will find that there is still plenty to do and the doing activates the power of attraction instead of promotion. Coast more, float more, enjoy more, and savor more. This is what it means to get more out of Life.

4. You Have a Wonderful Future

"I place the future in the hands of God." -A Course in Miracles

LIVING IN THE NOW does not in any way mean that you should not dream and vision a wonderful vital happy future for yourself. In fact, because of the way the human mind operates, most all humans are either looking forward to dreams, goals and happy visions of the future, or are visualizing and dreaming negative scenarios to terrify themselves. People need something to look forward to in life in order to summon more Life from the Cosmos.

In fact, one of the greatest problems among humans comes when people believe that they have no positive future to prepare for and no reason to dream or vision. It is an ancient truth that without vision the people will perish – and many perish internally long before the body passes away. When you stop dreaming, you start gradually leaving the planet.

Remember, your part is "what" not "how." Of course you don't know how your dreams can come true – that's not your part. Your part is to continue to joyfully expand your Consciousness with happy possibilities, even if they seem impossible to you. In fact, if they seem impossible to you but the dream itself brings you joy rather than frustration and hopelessness – well, these are the dreams it is most delightful for Us to Help you with. Your part is to HAPPILY vision. <u>Joy is the greatest magnet for the Law of Attraction to work with</u>. Happy visions come true because they are happy! They draw their own resources and opportunities to them.

This has nothing to do with "achieving" anything in the world, though that may happen. Some of your dreams may be about things like going to college, starting your own business, retiring early – but, We want you to also think in terms of looking forward to your summer garden, visiting the grandchildren, your morning hike in the canyon, taking the drive up the coast, sitting down with a good book on the weekend, and all the seemingly "little" things that make your heart sing and feed your soul.

Take little steps forward whenever possible, but all with non-attachment to the outcome. Of course not all of your dreams will come true – and as you grow in wisdom and experience you will be glad for this. And never forget, that even if a dream dies, you can always dream new dreams. And if you stay happy, non-attached and optimistic, the dreams themselves will lead you to wonderful experiences and people you would never have encountered otherwise. Dreaming is not about FORCING things to happen and it is not about making the mistake of thinking that happiness is in the future. Happiness is NOW, never in the future. <u>Happiness is the decision to take charge of your own mind while focusing on gratitude and appreciation</u>. Dream your future into existence one thought at a time, all while still placing the future in the hands of God.

5. You Are Multi-Dimensional

"The body cannot know. And while you limit your awareness to its tiny senses, you will not see the grandeur that surrounds you." -A Course in Miracles

NOT ONLY ARE YOU VIBRATIONAL BEINGS, you are also multi-dimensional beings existing on various planes simultaneously. It is only when you rigidly focus on the dense-seeming 3 dimensional plane that you are limited to body-identification. You have many bodies on many different dimensions – etheric bodies, bodies of Light and high-vibrational frequencies. You experience them regularly in the "Dreamtime" as you astrally travel in your sleep or during meditation and visioning.

The seemingly earth-bound body you may currently think of as yourself is a blessed manifestation of your Consciousness. <u>Never ever judge, curse or fear your body</u>. It is responding to your Consciousness and if you harbor attack thoughts, guilt, shame or blame about this body, it will seem to become denser because of your resistance. You can then feel "trapped" within a body because you are resisting and judging it. Instead, flood your body with Light every day in your meditations. Breathe in Light and begin to FEEL and sense that the "inner space" within it is expanding, that the cells are quickening with Divine Cosmic Wisdom. Remember, the body is not some ridiculous solid slab of meat you are dragging around the planet – in fact, it is mostly made up of empty space. The Universe is breathing you into existence every moment of every day throughout eternity and you must practice experiencing yourself as ONE with the Universe. You are not separate from anything.

It can be helpful if you begin first to think Fourth-Dimensionally. This Fourth Dimension is the State of Grace. In fact, many 3rd dimension problems are most easily solved and dissolved while you are thinking Fourth-Dimensionally. This is the space where you can feel Our Presence more easily – where you can receive guidance, direction and healings as you relax, relax, relax. To think 4th-Dimensionally, Consciously join Us here in the City of Light for some time each day by prayer, meditation or visualizing. You are already here vibrationally, but if you will simply REMEMBER this from time to time - if you will come here deliberately even for a moment or two by being AWARE of the Fourth-Dimension, you will find the miraculous manifestations and episodes of effortless accomplishment quicken substantially. You may begin to find that almost before you even perceive a need, it has been met. Cause and effect are experienced as nearly simultaneous happenings when you are in this Zone – which in Reality they are. But in the 3rd dimension the illusory time-gap seems longer if you are not Consciously visiting the Dreamtime for renewal and retreat.

In the Dreamtime, We are able to very Gracefully and easily download to you new Consciousness programs and even to make significant gentle changes to you on the cellular level. Again, breathing in Light and visioning your body being infused   until   you   see   it   glowing   with   sparkling phosphorescence that dissolves all resistance will significantly quicken your vibration as well as your manifestations of good. You will come to find that the more you relax, the better and clearer your manifestations will be and the fewer problems you will have to begin with.

Affirm for yourself frequently throughout the day:

*I am living in the State of Grace and
I am a being of Divine Light.*

6. A New Day!

"Decisions are continuous. You do not always know when you are making them. But with a little practice with the ones you recognize, a set begins to form which sees you through the rest. It is not wise to let yourself become preoccupied with every step you take. The proper set, adopted consciously each time you wake, will put you well ahead. And if you find resistance strong and dedication weak, you are not ready. Do not fight yourself. But think about the kind of day you want, and tell yourself there is a way in which this very day can happen just like that. Then try again to have the day you want." -A Course in Miracles

MY GOODNESS, HERE YOU ARE, back again. We so look forward to our time together everyday. Of course We are with you all the time and stand at the ready every moment to give as much Help as you will allow – but this is our special time in which you give us much more of your focus. We do not take for granted your attention and willingness to show up for what We have to share with you.

More than anything else, We are simply here to remind you of Who you are each day – and of what is possible for you.

We are here to remind you to open your Valve to the Flow of Divine Grace and to keep flowing positive energy and Light into all the aspects of your life. We are here to encourage, soothe, uplift, love and guide you. We are here to Help you never forget the JOY of daily living and to bring you back to peace when you get lost in endless thinking, thinking, thinking. We are here to gently remind you to lift up from whatever stressful story you may be telling yourself so that you can see the mountain, the flower, the puppy, the smiling baby, the sunset or any number of Divine Creations that will bring you back to Self.

There is love and beauty all around you – there is kindness, gentleness and Grace. There are wonderful people and infinite possibilities for happy connections. This day need not be *"same old, same old"* if YOU are WILLING to see things with a little more wonder and appreciation today. You get to choose. You may focus on what is missing and what has been lost, or you can focus on the grandeur and simple beauty of what is here and what may yet come. We stand ready to Help you at every turn if you will ask and allow. There are no words to let you know how much we love and enjoy you – what a kick we get out of you and what a delight you are to Us! We never judge you. You do not frustrate Us in the least. We have infinite patience and love when it comes to you.

Now, what would you like to come of this day? What do you want to bring to it and what would you like to get out of it? How may we Help you today?

7. Marry Yourself

"And so they wander through a world of strangers, unlike themselves, living with their bodies perhaps under a common roof that shelters neither; in the same room and yet a world apart. A holy relationship starts from a different premise. Each one has looked within and seen no lack. Accepting his completion, he would extend it by joining with another, whole as himself."

-A Course in Miracles

YOU ARE GOING TO BE WITH YOU for all of eternity. There is no way for you to ever escape yourself. Wherever you go, there you are. And until you can make peace with yourself, it will be nearly impossible to make peace with anyone else. Too often relationships in your world are used as an attempt to get away from yourself by "joining" with another. This is merely a distraction. Relationships between two whole beings are delicious and can be very fruitful – between those who feel incomplete; they can be very messy and even quite destructive.

We suggest that regardless of whether you ever marry another person or not, that you marry yourself as well. Too often humans treat themselves like a roommate they have at least mild contempt for – looking in the mirror and calling her fat, old, lazy and stupid – doing things just to make her shut up or to placate her – indulging her rather than actually cherishing her and giving her something of true value.

Remember, the seeming world outside of you will treat you the way you treat yourself. YOU are the one who sets the tone and leads the way. No one can give you what you are unwilling to give yourself. Someone can tell you all day long how wonderful, limitless, beautiful, capable and brilliant you are, but until YOU are willing to BELIEVE it and say it to yourself, their words will be like booze to an alcoholic – it will never satisfy or quench you and you will just want more and more and more.

To marry yourself requires no ceremony but it might be very helpful for you to write vows just the same. Take yourself to have and to hold, to love and honor, to walk with and support all the days of this life and beyond. Begin to romance and woo yourself daily as you would someone you met whom you wanted to have an intimate loving relationship with – never criticize or condemn. Never withhold or lie to – and never give up on. Treat yourself as the valuable treasure you would want a "soul-mate" to – and never settle for less from yourself.

The fact is, you are in a LONG-term committed relationship whether you have wanted to admit it or not. Now the question is, what have you been committed to doing? Hare you browbeating, judging, punishing, pushing, and resisting yourself? <u>You ARE your soul-mate. No one is coming along to save you or to complete you</u>. In fact, you don't need saving, but you may need to recognize that what you've been seeking has been here all along. Call off the search. Bring in the dogs. Let the honeymoon begin.

8. Coming From a Loving Place

"Teach only love, for that is what you are." -A Course in Miracles

LOVE IS WHAT YOU ARE. Love is what created you. Love is what heals, restores and renews. Love is sanity in the midst of the storm. <u>When you are not coming from love, you</u>

are not being yourself. Therefore, your job each day is to come from a loving place by opening your heart, particularly in all the moments which seem like they have nothing at all to do with love.

Getting caught up in the "stories" of your day is what keeps you from coming from a loving place. The fearful part of the mind gathers evidence of why love is impractical, or foolish. It gathers up evidence of how unlovable or unworthy the other is . . . or how unlovable and unworthy you are. Remember, this fearful part of the mind will even convince you that you are very actively seeking for love, even as it continues to gather up evidence and builds a case about how love in this situation is simply not possible or reasonable. It will build a case for the "laws" of scarcity and finite resources. It will tell you that love is weakness and vulnerability. This is perhaps the greatest lie of all for love is the ONLY true strength and invulnerability in the entire Universe.

Coming from a loving place is not about what you DO in the external necessarily, but it IS about what you DO in terms of keeping your heart soft and open. It does not mean that you always say yes – it does not mean that you become a doormat, lend them money, go into business with them, or do anything else that your gut tells you not to. Remember, coming from a love place means toward the other AND toward yourself. The Holy Spirit's solutions are always win/win! This is what true Prayer is for – to turn within and seek Divine Guidance.

It is unloving to yourself to go over to pet the dog that bites you every time. Love is not about close proximity. You can love the dog from the comfort of your own yard. Love does not demand hugs or physical presence. Love is thinking kind and gentle thoughts – giving mercy and understanding, and yes, forgiveness. Forgive yourself. Forgive the other. And keep on turning up the vibration of love pouring out of your heart-center. <u>You can deny someone your company without denying them your love, just as you can go to lunch with someone and judge them the entire time</u>. Love is not about the body.

Let this become a Guiding Light for you – a part of your Spiritual Guidance System each day as you GENTLY check in frequently with yourself to see,

> *"Am I coming from a loving place right now?"*

9. Real Change

"The peace of God is everything I want. The peace of God is my one goal; the aim of all my living here, the end I seek, my purpose and my function and my life, while I abide here where I am not at home." -A Course in Miracles

CAN YOU UNDERSTAND THE POWER OF THESE WORDS and the limitless comfort they will give you if you can say and MEAN them? <u>Think of all the shabby substitutes that you have sought after and accepted in place of the peace of God</u>. Make that useless journey no more.

Today you can ACCEPT the peace of God and leave your suffering behind. The peace of God is not a "religious" state available only to those who have moved to a monastery or nunnery. It is not a dull static state of emotionless detachment from life. The peace of God is joyful beyond measure. This peace has nothing to do with your earthly roles and is equally available to the mother, politician, movie star, barista, lawyer and corporate CEO. You may accept the peace of God while living in a mansion or living in your car - whether your body is young and strong or broken and bent with disease. There are no special or chosen people when it comes to the peace of God.

What is required is the willingness to exchange all that the world has taught you to value in order to accept this peace. This is an inner experience. It does not mean that you *"get rid of"* anything for that is usually just an opposing belief in the power of the external to affect you. It is an exchanging of one value system for one which is entirely different than your own. It is an inner shift which may leave your life looking EXACTLY the same as it did before the shift happened. But YOU will be different - your energy and the amount of Light that you are able to channel will change.

So then the question is, do you want ONLY the peace of God? Or is there something else that you still think you can use to barter with or chase after in hopes that it can offer you something better?

10. Try Softer

"It is only because you think you can run some small part or deal with certain aspects of your life alone, that the guidance of the Holy Spirit is limited." -A Course in Miracles

YOU ARE RAISED UP TO BELIEVE that all "failure" can be avoided or overcome if you will only buckle down and try HARDER - work harder at achieving your goal. You are hypnotized into a painful thought system which teaches that you must CONQUER life and MAKE LIFE work for you through your struggle, efforting and steely determination. In this philosophy, the ultimate goal is simply getting your own way, in whatever area of life you are focused on.

Where is the joy in this stressful mythology? Where is the peace? Where is the love? Well, there really is no time for those things when you are busy, busy, busy trying harder and harder to work an unworkable plan. And it is unworkable mostly because forcing life to turn out YOUR way is building your house on sand. Whatever you FORCED into working, you will have to continue to WORK HARD to maintain. There is no rest within this insane thought system. There is motivation, but no inspiration.

There IS another way. There is a path of joy, peace and love in which you do not try harder - you try softer. You don't force, you allow. You don't demand, you invite. You don't motivate, you inspire. You don't follow your plan - you follow your joy. You don't tell God what to do, you ask that your mind be healed and made sane. <u>It is not a path of endless competition but of invigorating cooperation</u>. Basically, it's heaven on earth, right here and right now.

So start to practice this softness if Heaven appeals to you. The next time things seems to be slipping out of your "control," instead of desperately trying harder and harder to regain control, take a few moments to get quiet inside, to breathe and relax and let all the thoughts begin to slow down. Then, replace the old trying harder with trying softer. Become gentle in your thinking and in your approach.

11. That's For Me!

"You who are sometimes sad and sometimes angry; who sometimes feel your just due is not given you, and your best efforts meet with lack of appreciation and even contempt; give up these foolish thoughts! They are too small and meaningless to occupy your holy mind an instant longer." -A Course in Miracles

THE THINGS OF THE PHYSICAL WORLD can never content you, satisfy you or make you happy. They hold out promises that they cannot keep. You must have at least suspected this by now. Chasing after the meaningless will never bring you the joy that you seek. However, renunciation and aversion to the things of the world is the exact same mistake because it places your joy in mere symbols. Therefore, if there is something you wish to be, do or have – as long as it does not rob another, there is no reason for you to not go for it. Let Us Help you not only in the process, but also in remembering that your joy is NOW, whether you ever achieve your goal or not. This is called non-attachment to outcomes.

Too often you look out at your world and think that others have some special "in" which opens doors for them that seem closed to you. You still believe too much in finite resources and special people. In essence, you sometimes believe more in luck than in the Universal Spiritual Laws. You believe in HARD work and struggle more than in a loving Universe that is based on matching frequencies and Consciousness. In time, this can lead to bitterness and hardness of heart . . . and certainly to depression.

But We are here to bring you good tidings of great JOY! We are here to remind you of the Laws of Consciousness – and to Help you begin to raise your frequency so that you will be a match to the things you would like to be, do, have or experience. Of course this does not mean that you will "get" everything you want because that in itself can be disastrous. But you CAN experience much more than you currently believe, BY changing what you believe, one thought at a time.

The first step is to let go of the idea of finite resources and limited good. It begins by aligning yourself with possibilities instead of "probabilities." It begins with the statement *"That's for me!"* We invite you to begin to look around your world and focus on the people, places, things and experiences that activate your JOY – and instead of starting to strategize about how to "get" them or making up negative stories about people who have them, you simply say, "That's for me!" This is a statement that tells your subconscious mind that what one person has, you can have too. If one person has ever healed from a disease, you can too. If one person has ever started their own business, you can too! If one person has ever gotten married at age 75, you can too! If one person has ever paid off all their debts, you can too! That's you for if YOU say so! No one is stopping you but you, and some ridiculous story in your head.

Begin today to end all stories of self-pity and martyrdom as you begin to gleefully walk around your world seeing all the wonderful experiences available as you remind yourself frequently, "That's for me too!"

12. Deal With It & Turn It Around

"What fear has hidden still is part of you. Joining the Atonement is the way out of fear. The Holy Spirit will help you reinterpret everything that you perceive as fearful, and teach you that only what is loving is true." -A Course in Miracles

FEAR IS LIKE A VIRUS that infects your mental/emotional hard drive. It runs quietly in the background infecting as many files as possible without notice. It infects them with small fear-based thoughts that you read in the newspaper or see on television. It comes from snippets of conversations here and there or from pictures you don't even consciously remember seeing in a magazine. It may come as a faint memory that plays in the distant background – perhaps something that was said to you when you were a small child. It can even be a "motivating" slogan which is actually causing you tremendous stress and pressure to perform - something as simple and yet relentlessly stressful as *"living your best life."*

Your system very gradually starts running more slowly, getting more sluggish for seemingly no reason. You feel irritated or lonely from out of nowhere - and yet nothing in your external life has really changed much if at all. Everything just feels different, and not in a good way. Little illnesses and aches and pains start to arise. People are starting to bother you because they breathe too loud. Things begin to feel overwhelming at times - even simple things. And now you start WISHING instead of choosing. Eventually, left unchecked and not dealt with, the small fears will become overwhelming fears, panic, defensiveness, depression, rage and so much more. It will crash the system.

The ONLY power the fear virus has is that it is HIDDEN and you are not aware of it. It is actually a very weak virus and that is why it must remain hidden - because it is so easily swept away once you are onto it. It is the ONLY virus that exists. There are no others.

You think you are angry, but you are afraid. You think you are depressed, but you are afraid. You think you are impatient, but you are afraid. You think you are frustrated, but you are afraid. You think you are lonely, but you are afraid. You think you are anxious, but you are afraid. You think you have many different problems, but you only have one. The problem is fear.

It is good to do a weekly virus scan. You merely sit down with paper and a pen and go inside to scan for any fears that have come up as you put them down on paper. Write at the top of the page "Virus Scan" and then list whatever uncomfortable thoughts or feelings that you sense within or that appears in mind regardless of what words you use. Don't be spiritual or poetic. Just vomit it all out on paper. Let the ego have its say on paper where it cannot hurt you or anyone else. Be as petty or judgmental or unspiritual as you feel in that moment. Some weeks there may be a lot - other weeks practically nothing at all.

When you've gotten it out on paper, it's time to move it to the trash file to be deleted. One way to do this is to turn it over to Us as your Cosmic Office Manager to deal with. You may choose to write a prayer of surrendering it all to God:

> *Dear God, I surrender all these lies of the ego to You to evaporate back into nothingness. I release them to you fully and freely now and am rebooted to my Original Self as You programmed me to be!"*

You can also take those thoughts and turn them around to Prayer Treatment Affirmations. A thought like, *"I'm getting weak and haggard and my body is falling apart"* can become, "THE CELLS OF MY BODY ARE DIVINE INTELLIGENCE ITSELF AND THEY KNOW WHAT TO DO TO RENEW AND REVITALIZE THEMSELVES EACH DAY. SPIRIT RUNS MY BODY AND I BLESS MY BODY WITH LOVE AND APPRECIATION." A fear thought like, *"I'm afraid my savings are going to run out and I'm going to end up losing everything and living on the streets"* can become, "GOD IS MY REFUGE AND SECURITY AND GOD GOES WITH ME EVERYWHERE I GO. I AM SAFE AND I HAVE DIVINE WISDOM GUIDING ME TO RIGHT THOUGHTS AND RIGHT ACTIONS. LIFE LOVES ME AND I KNOW THAT DOORS ARE OPENING NOW FOR MY INCREASED GOOD IN ALL ASPECTS OF LIVING."

If you take this little once-a-week action to deal with any hidden thoughts or secret beliefs that have crept into your mind, you will find that it SAVES you tremendous time each and every day because your operating system will be running at optimum efficiency. That is what the Atonement is for - it is the ultimate virus scan that detects and wipes clean any corrupted files and puts them back to factory settings of the perfect Child of God.

Don't make a big deal out of this process. Pay MUCH MORE attention to your daily affirmative prayers, spiritual reading, doing lists of positive aspects, gratitude lists, words of praise, savoring and expecting only good. But it is a very good idea to take time once a week, for even 10 minutes, to do virus scan to see if any resentments, grievances, guilt, shame, anger, attack and such have crept into your mind so that you can easily sweep them out with the Atonement Program Fear Virus Scanning System. It is only what you keep hidden from yourself that can really hurt you because you've made it inaccessible to the Atonement Principle. Get it up and out quickly and move onto enJOYing a life in which you are under no laws but God's.

13. Feed the Champion

"What fear would feed upon, love overlooks. What fear demands, love cannot even see." -A Course in Miracles

FEEDING THE CHAMPION. It is good for you to stop and acknowledge just how far you have come in these lessons by feeding your inner champion. You are continually learning not to feed the ego, which is the inner bully, and have instead begun the excellent habit of feeding your true Self, the champion within you. What is actually happening in this process is that you are changing and refining your appetites.

However, it will do little good if you think of these spiritual boot camps as something you do for a while to clean up your vibration and then you just go right back to your old ways as soon as it is over. This would be like saying, *"Well, I brushed my teeth so thoroughly and completely this morning that I don't think I will ever need to do it again!"* <u>Backsliding can happen very quickly without proper attention and diligence.</u>

The purpose of these boot camps is to instill new habits which create an energetic momentum that will continue to reap rewards and benefits for as long as you continue putting energy into it each day - even long after the boot camp is completed. The difference is that when you begin a new way of thinking and living it takes a much greater effort because you are changing the direction of the inertia. You'd been going in one direction and are now turning around to go in the opposite direction. Now that you've been going in this new direction for some time, it takes much less energy to continue going forward.

When you were being taught to brush your teeth as a small child, perhaps you had to be nagged by your parents to do it. It took a lot of energy to ingrain the habit. It was a decision that you had to be endlessly reminded of making each day. But by now, there is no decision to make. You don't DECIDE whether you will brush your teeth each day. You just do it because it's a habit. <u>Thinking is a habit too. Your thoughts are mental habit patterns which you learned - and you can and are learning new ones</u>. Many of them have already started to take root in you and to bear good fruit.

BUT DO NOT GET LAZY AND SLOPPY about this or you may find that you have once again started feeding those old ego fear-driven thoughts and concepts. Some time each and every day must be spent feeding and nourishing the champion within. A champion requires good quality nutrition in order to meet each challenge of the day and even in order to simply rest in JOY.

So the question each day becomes, *"What am I feeding the Champion today?"*

14. *Soothe and Uplift Yourself Daily*

"Every thought you think and every word you speak is an affirmation." - Louise L. Hay

IT IS NOT YOUR ROLE TO MAKE THINGS HAPPEN but merely to line up with Who you really are. You must remember that while the world can be a hostile place, the Universe is a very friendly place. You are not a child of this world. You are a child of the Universe. Do not forget this.

One of your main problems is that you often line up with your perceived limitations rather than lining up with your Greater Self. You do this through your own inner conversation as well as in your outer conversation. You casually throw away your good by lining up with the hostile world instead of lining up with your Infinite Friend.

Every limiting story you tell about the past, present or future activates that same limiting vibration within you and keeps you in that old energy pattern. Every time you whine, criticize, bemoan, grumble, murmur and complain you are BLOCKING and DENYING your own good by AFFIRMING LIMITATION. That means your good has to keep on circling the airport because you have not provided the place for it to land.

Do you understand that this is all there is for you to do, create a space for your good to land? And all of this is happening INSIDE OF YOU. It is circling around WITHIN YOU - you don't even have to look "out there" for it to come from "outer space" or your old mythical religious Santa Claus God.

You must practice sowing seeds in your life through your WORDS. You need not speak the most positive amazing life-affirming words anyone has ever said. You need only speak words that encourage, soothe and uplift even slightly and this will start activating the higher vibrations within you. You don't need to reach for something AMAZINGLY positive to think or say if that is not yet how you feel. Start where you are and just begin a gently stretching.

If you are terrified about your dwindling finances and haven't been able to find work for some time, you don't need to affirm, *"I have an amazing job with piles of money filling my bank accounts"* because that is usually too far vibrationally from where you currently are and can just make you more tense. Go easy and gentle - soothe yourself into a higher vibration:

> *"I have some wonderful skills and I know that I can be a good addition to the right company. There are companies that are looking for someone just like me right now and we're being drawn together by Source. I am available for the right company and it's going to be a great fit for us both. I can enjoy this time off because I know that soon I'll be busy working every day with wonderful people. Lots can happen and the Universe has not lost my file."*

You can massage your thoughts to a place where you are continually lining up with your own greater good. Start right where you are and just keep reaching for the thoughts that feel good when you think them, the words that feel good when you say them.

15. Do Your Best in THIS Moment

"And if you find resistance strong and dedication weak, you are not ready. Do not fight yourself." -A Course in Miracles

IF YOU COULD LEARN TO GIVE YOURSELF A BREAK, you would be much more willing to do the same for others and your life in general would be so much more pleasant and filled with love. Understand that this is not about allowing your ego to make excuses for you but rather it is about understanding the flow of energies. Your energies rise and fall throughout the day as well as throughout the weeks, months and years.

Your best is different when you are sick than it is when you are vibrantly healthy. It is different when you are depressed than when you are joyous. It is different when you are stressed out than when you are focused and peaceful. Learn to become aware of your energy as it is - learn how to work with it so that you can do whatever is your best at THAT moment rather than comparing it with a different "better" or "worse" moment.

Let go of feeling defensive or guilty and simply do your best in THIS moment, just as it is and just as YOU are. What others think about your best is not your concern. Their thoughts about your best are only projections about themselves anyhow so stay in your own yard. Be gently yet totally honest with yourself so that you are not copping out on yourself nor pushing yourself too hard. HONOR whatever is your best in this moment and give it willingly to whatever you are doing. Doing your best need not be INTENSE and SERIOUS. It IS focused but there can also be a graceful absence of struggle. Struggle is usually the result of fighting against the energies that are present at the moment - trying to

FORCE them to change. This is war.

It may seem strange to you (as most Truth does) but doing your best feels almost effortless and relaxing because it is about a deep self-acceptance as you put one foot in front of the other. Remember that doing your best is not about external outcomes. The one thing that you <u>can</u> do the very best is to be YOU - to bring your true self to whatever task is in front of you - to be authentically yourself even as you walk to the mailbox or make yourself a sandwich. It's not about doing BIG important things in the world but rather about the energy you bring to anything. So even if your best today is to lie in bed all day resting and recovering, that is absolutely wonderful and holy and blessed!

16. Where Are You Going?

"If a man does not know what harbor he is making for, no wind is the right wind." -Seneca

MANY TIMES YOU GET SO CAUGHT UP in "dealing with" whatever is happening in your now that you lose track of where you are heading and why you are heading there. This tends to lead to overwhelm, boredom and eventually even despair. It is essential that you look forward because energy is always moving and there is nothing that is truly standing still. ENERGY MOVES.

When driving your car you look out the windshield so you'll know how to proceed. You are both fully in your NOW, but also giving great attention to where you are going. If you give 100% of your attention to your now, just gazing around within the car, you will crash and burn. If you focus entirely on the road ahead and your destination, you will be impatient, anxious and not enjoy the trip. Your attention needs to be somewhat balanced.

Additionally, if you are only focused on "dealing with" whatever is in front of you today, because attention is creative, through the law of attraction you will be creating more of whatever you are dealing with. And when We say that you must be looking forward, We don't mean to some HUGE future event that you are preparing for - it can be something as simple as preparing to enjoy a wonderful dinner with loved ones. It could be seeing your child graduate from college that you are looking forward to - or to running that 5K, or spending time in the garden in the summer.

Attention and Intention - very important. You must give the Universe something to work with consciously or you will do it unconsciously. And make sure you put JOY in there. A joyful journey has a joyous ending for means and end are ONE. Make your goals, intentions, objectives and destinations FUN rather than serious and significant. Remember, learning is meant to be joyful.

17. Affirmative Prayer: Treatment

"Prayer is the medium of miracles." -A Course in Miracles

PETITIONARY PRAYER IS NOT MUCH BETTER than merely wishing or hoping. Beseeching some authority figure up in the sky to send help is not much more than superstition relating more to Santa Claus than to the actual God-Source.

There is not a God - but there is God. That God is as indwelling as It is outer and there is no place where God-Source is not. Therefore, God is not beseeched or implored but rather ACTIVATED either consciously or unconsciously. Affirmative Prayer, or Treatment, is one powerful way of CONSCIOUSLY activating God-Source and DIRECTING that power . . . from WITHIN you.

An Affirmative Prayer Treatment is something as

simple and powerful as, *"I always have what I need."* Hundreds of the workbook lessons of the Course are Affirmative Prayer Treatments, such as,

> *"I am under no laws but God's. Your grace is given me. I claim it now. I am not weak but strong. God is with me. I live and move in Him. I am in danger nowhere in the world. I am surrounded by the love of God. My present happiness is all I see."*

These are all generalized treatments - very powerful. And you can go much more specific,

> *"Joyous opportunities for employment are seeking and finding me now. My body knows how to heal itself as I peacefully sleep. My relationships are loving, balanced and harmonious. I am attracting wonderful new friends for activities we love to do together."*

And on it goes.

Treatment sets LAW into motion. It is not passive or wishy-washy. It does not rely on hopes or wishes or a fictional man in the sky to come save you. YOU save yourself because you have been given the tools - your own mind and the power of your word!

18. Leave Your Nets

"You are not bereft of help, and Help that knows the answer. Would you be content with little, which is all that you alone can offer yourself, when He Who gives you everything will simply offer it to you? He will never ask what you have done to make you worthy of the gift of God. Ask it not therefore of yourself. Instead, accept His answer, for He knows that you are worthy of everything God wills for you." -A Course in Miracles

STRAIN, STRUGGLE, STRIVING, suffering, strategizing . . . these are all the ridiculous ways the ego tries to tell you that creativity is born and solutions are arrived at. It is yet another lie formulated to make you suffer. Surely you must see how "brainstorming" is largely an egoic pastime. Why would you CHOOSE to create a storm in your already anxious brain? "*Racking your brain*" is another totally insane attempt at figuring out HOW you can FORCE yourself into the realm of solutions. This is madness. Yet in your world these things are actively encouraged and even celebrated. They have nothing to do with Reality or true success.

True Answers and creativity come when the mind is relaxed, open and spacious. Remember that you are NOT alone. You have Help that KNOWS the Answer to everything that ever confronts you if you will simply calm down enough to LISTEN and ACCEPT the Answers even though they may not fit your picture of what the perfect answer looks like.

To "*leave your nets*" is to let go of all your strategies of how to get what you think you want and need. It is to TRUST that We know what you need even before you do. When Brother Jesus told the apostles to leave their nets he was telling them to release their old attachments to outer ways of getting their needs met and to trust in the Divine Consciousness instead.

We DO understand how terrifying this can be for you at times. But doesn't it also feel TRUE to you – doesn't it soothe your soul? Does it not resonate with the very cells of your body as Truth? And We also understand how difficult it can be to let go of manipulation, control, and strategizing since your whole world is actively encouraging you to TAKE CONTROL of the outer world through these tools. Whereas We are actively encouraging you to TAKE CONTROL of your inner world by marinating in the Kingdom Within.

We are always Helping you, but We want you to consider this time in your life as a Spiritual Intensive Workshop in which your Consciousness is being GENTLY and joyfully expanded to do the work for you. Your part is to FOCUS your imagination on that which fills you with joy, peace, love, enthusiasm, serenity and positive expectancy. Worry is nothing more than negative use of the imagination and expecting the worst. Your job now is simply to do the opposite of that. Instead of racking your brain, massage it. Instead of brainstorming, try some brain soothing.

We have MANY gifts to give you in the coming days and the more calm, open and receptive you are, the greater the gifts will be.

19. Fear Not

"You may still complain about fear, but you nevertheless persist in making yourself fearful." -A Course in Miracles

MANY SCRIPTURES ARE FULL OF ADMONITIONS to *"fear not"* and *"be not afraid."* This is Our constant attempt to remind you that fear is under your own control. YOU are the one terrifying yourself with your own thoughts because your mind is so undisciplined. In fact, many of you actually seek out terrifying information on television, newspapers, magazines, talk shows, and even in casual conversations with people - then you claim that you are anxious and depressed because of a *"chemical imbalance"* or you blame something in the foods you are eating. This is typical of the ego's plan for salvation, which is all about holding grievances and projecting guilt onto the outer world.

But this need not be. There is nothing to fear. Fear is nothing more than another mental habit which has been unconsciously cultivated and tolerated. We have been attempting in Our various writings to you to soothe you into the place of allowing all things to work for your good without your fear, resistance, micro-managing, worrying and struggling. LIFE LOVES YOU and there is a perfect Divine Plan for every child of God. The Plan is for your perfect happiness - period. God has not lost your file . . . but you have often actively interfered and drastically slowed down the Divine Plan with your own fears and strategies.

All We really ask of you is that each morning, as soon after waking as possible, that you spend some time with Us in communion. Speak to Us in honesty and frankness, give Us your burdens and tell us your intentions for the day . . . then LISTEN as We give you directions and Help on what to think and sometimes even what to do. Fear not. We are with you. You are not alone. All truly IS well with you. There is so much more good to come - but only to the degree that you can relax and let it in.

20. There Is Nothing Wrong With You

"Nor is a lifetime of contemplation and long periods of meditation aimed at detachment from the body necessary. All such attempts will ultimately succeed because of their purpose. Yet the means are tedious and very time consuming, for all of them look to future for release from a state of present unworthiness and inadequacy. Your way will be different, not in purpose but in means." -A Course in Miracles

YOU WOULD DO WELL TO STOP "working on" yourself and abandon the idea of "self-improvement" entirely and for all time. These attempts are rooted in a mistaken assumption to begin with - therefore, it will lead you on endless journeys to nowhere. There is only one thing that needs to be changed, and that is your mind. EVERYTHING comes from this. And without this change, every other seeming change is temporary at best. Your mistaken assumption is that you NEED improvement and fixing - that you need to GET something or figure something out or dramatically alter who you are. This is how ego controls you and keeps you filled with stress and anxiety. THIS is what must be changed - this insane notion.

Begin with the realization that there is absolutely nothing wrong with you - you are not broken or wounded, you do not need to be fixed or healed. It is only mind that needs any healing . . . and even that is not literally true. It is true that you have been through some disturbing things, have made mistakes, have fallen down, have acted out - but these are all behaviors and have nothing to do with your essential Self. Your essential Self remains as it was created by God and nothing you have ever done, thought, failed to do, or not thought, has changed that self. You cannot improve upon perfection.

Relax and be who you are. Being gets lost in "becoming." You tend to want to become rather than to BE. You are far too mentally intense and this makes you emotionally intense. Your mind gets all tied up in knots over nothing. This makes you get very excited with every new worldly plan which involves you finally "*getting your act together*" and solving all your problems. In fact, it is only the perception that there IS a problem which is the problem. A complicated mind creates complicated situations - then you blame the situation for how you feel and think that you need a miracle to change the situation or to change your basic personality. It is only mind that needs changing - not through adding more complicated theories, but through an undoing process - a letting go of all attempts to fix.

Let your shoulders drop . . . relax and unclench your jaw . . . take a deep breath . . . relax the forehead and the tongue and the eyes . . . nice soft belly . . . relax the buttocks and sink down into where you are sitting as you let go of all tension, anxiety and worry. There is nothing wrong with you. There is nothing to get, or fix, or change . . . there is just this gentle opening to receive.

21. Simple Miracles

"The use of miracles as spectacles to induce belief is a misunderstanding of their purpose." -A Course in Miracles

AS YOU READ THESE LESSONS you are opening up your energy centers to allow Us to Help along your healing through the Grace of God. The words We use here are the ideal vibrational choice for Us to begin to reorganize even the very cells of your body to a state of wholeness and balance. It is YOUR Consciousness which is doing this, not Ours. We are merely like a tuning fork and you are matching the Cosmic Tones We are sounding. We are not so much working ON you as working WITH you by the Signal We are transmitting and you are receiving. None of this is happening from outside of you, or from "up there" except in the sense that these are higher Frequencies and States within you.

And please remember, We are not drama angels. Most of Our work is done on the subtle levels where We help you solve problems before they even manifest in form - you are not even aware of them. Some of you have had "major illnesses" forming in your body which were dissipated vibrationally before there was even the first symptom felt. The dis-ease was gradually released as We kept guiding your thoughts and emotions to the place of sanity, peace and joy.

Have you not noticed at times how much more smoothly everything seems to go for you now when you spend some time with Us? Simple and smooth is Our way. Those of you still attracted to drama, quantum leaps, huge epiphanies, mania and despair, and the "excitement" of the ego storyline . . . well, your issue is mainly that you are still in the phase of what the Course calls, "*the desire to get rid of peace.*" But not to worry, if you keep showing up and shutting up, that will pass too. Remember, peace and joy are not boring in the least, but it can take time for some of you to let your nervous systems shift to a less dense way of perceiving.

We seldom go for the BIG miracles because they bring too much of the wrong kind of attention, interest and motivation. And usually they tend to be temporary because there is often not the "*mental equivalency*" to maintain them long term.

Since each day should be devoted to miracles, begin by KNOWING that they are happening all the time - you merely need practice in recognizing them. So again, slow down, breathe, relax and look around. Right where you are at this exact moment there are many many miracles — however, you may need to put on your rose colored glasses to see them. Trust Us, you will find whatever you are looking for, whether it is evidence of miracles or evidence of darkness. YOU are the one who chooses - either deliberately or by default. Make the better choice today dear one. We are with you.

22. Relax Into The Divine

"Why would you struggle so frantically to anticipate all you cannot know, when all knowledge lies behind every decision the Holy Spirit makes for you?" –A Course in Miracles

TRUE HEALING IS THE RESULT OF SURRENDER, more than the result of *"winning the war"* against any illness or condition. Healing is realignment with Source. Healing is remembering that of yourself, you can do nothing - and what is more, you don't even know what the best outcome would be. The Surrender We speak of, is a surrender to Trust and Grace. And though of yourself you can do nothing to heal yourself, you CAN ALLOW healing to BE. Healing is natural and normal. It is the way of the Universe. It is not the way of war, but of peace.

Remember little miracle-worker, you are never separate from the One Who loves you beyond all measure. There is a good plan for your life and the plan is for your perfect happiness. The plan is not about where you will live or what you will do so much as it is about Guiding you to a state of forever being reminded of the Infinite Oneness of which you are a part. NOTHING can separate you from the Whole. Right where you are at this very moment, you are held perfectly in the Hands of God and all is well.

Stress, fear, anxiety and tension are merely the signs to show you that you are thinking or believing something that is not in alignment with Truth. You are judging by appearances or more so, by an extremely limited nightmarish illusion of the appearances. It is your interpretation of circumstances which causes this stress and suffering. Let it go dear one. You KNOW Us by now. Have We not been true to you? Have We not walked you through every dark night in order to show you that the darkness holds nothing at all?

Your job is to go within frequently throughout each day to remember the Divine Source. It need only be an instant, one moment at the top of each hour in which you take mere seconds to close your eyes, breathe deeply and say to yourself, *"All things are held perfectly in the hands of God"* or some other thought which soothes you in your downstream journey. Do not deny yourself the JOY that comes from frequent Conscious Contact.

Give up your struggle today as you allow <u>THE</u> PLAN to replace your plan. Remember, in the Divine Plan you are on a "need-to-know" basis. Release the past and let go of the future and you will find that TODAY holds all that you need to be happy, joyous, carefree and peaceful as you place the future in the hands of God.

23. Be Kind

"If you point out the errors of your brother's ego you must be seeing through yours, because the Holy Spirit does not perceive his errors . . . When you react at all to errors, you are not listening to the Holy Spirit. He has merely disregarded them, and if you attend to them you are not hearing Him." -A Course In Miracles

A S OUR BROTHER KEN HAS SAID, you could boil the entire Course down to two words: BE KIND.

It is not surprising that the ego uses New Thought, metaphysics and the Course as a weapon because it will use whatever is necessary to have you focus on guilt in yourself or project it onto another. The ego has merely dressed up the concept of sin in sheep's clothing with words like error and used them in the exact same mistaken way. It is a form of disguised attack.

MANY sick minds are housed in extremely healthy bodies. And many living Masters lived in "crippled" sickly bodies. The body is nothing. It means nothing. It is neutral.

When you "diagnose" metaphysical error you are really looking for sin. When you point out to another their "error" you are attacking him and calling him sinful, even when you use the words of the Course to do so. *"How did you create this illness? What do you think this is about?"* or even *"How did I create this illness?"* is merely an attack and the search for sin unless the patient has **SPECIFICALLY ASKED what you think, see or sense**. To do so without this specific asking is completely wrong and makes CERTAIN that NO HEALING can take place. You CANNOT focus on error/sin and then heal it. They are totally opposite frequencies. ONLY LOVE CAN HEAL. BE KIND rather than clever. Shift the vibration and you shift the effects. Look not to error but only to energy and vibrations.

When the (often mistaken) apostles asked Jesus in regards to the blind man, *"Master, who did sin, this man, or his parents, that he was born blind?"* he replied, *"neither."* No error was seen by the Master Teacher and neither should one be seen by you if you would be a Spiritually Mature Miracle Worker! You will not heal nor perform miracles by diagnosing or by studying error of any kind at any time. You heal by overlooking the error ENTIRELY and extending ONLY kindness and love - whether that love is a word, a hug, a touch, a thought, a pill, an ointment or anything else the patient is ready to receive.

No one really wants your good advice and clever insights. They are usually ego-based. Your kind and loving thoughts will heal. Seeing the Strength in one who is weak is what heals. Staying humble and silent is usually the best way. In no instant of healing did Brother Jesus say more than a sentence or two, which had nothing whatsoever to do with taking a family history, or asking anything more than, *"Do you want to be healed?"*

You are not the healer but merely the one who can allow healing to be. You heal not by your words, but by activating the vibration of love and acceptance, while overlooking all supposed "errors" - and in that, healing happens, even if the healing is that the body "dies." THERE IS NO DEATH, only the dropping of the body! Remember, the body represents nothing whatsoever whether it is "sick" or "well" - the Healer is not looking to the body for evidence of anything. Do your work, and then let it go COMPLETELY. Then you too may say, *"I did nothing. Your faith has made you whole."*

24. *Healing is Making Happy*

"You still have too much faith in the body as a source of strength . . . There is one thing that you have never done; you have not utterly forgotten the body . . . Love knows no bodies, and reaches to everything created like itself." -A Course In Miracles

T HE CONDITION OF THE BODY is no more a sign of healing than houses, property and cash are a sign of true wealth. The entire world you see is backward, upside down and inside out. You look to the finite to find the infinite - and you are disappointed time after time by the emptiness and seeming loss.

Yet every moment is an opportunity to repent. To "repent" means to turn around. You are facing the wrong direction, going the wrong way. Have you not noticed how often the more you "work" on something the worse it tends to get? This is because when you focus on fixing rather than appreciating, you are actually increasing the mental equivalency of "broken." The worse it gets, the worse it gets.

And have you not noticed that in moments when you become quite distracted from the problem, in that moment it ceases to be? You may have a severe toothache, but if you drop a brick on your bare foot you may become so distracted by the pain in your foot that your tooth stops hurting entirely. You may have heard that "*laughter is the best medicine*" or have read of one of your earthly teachers who taught of healing his dis-ease through watching comedies on television. A joyful distraction allows matter to balance and adjust ITSELF.

Now, if you TELL someone to forget their dis-ease, all you have done is made them MORE AWARE of the dis-ease and you are actually beating the drum which keeps it activated within them. "*To heal is to make happy*" is all you need remember. But you cannot give what you do not have. You must BE happy to bring happiness. Begin there, one happy thought at a time - even if it is only SLIGHTLY happy compared to the previous thoughts. Start where you are. Soothe yourself to a better-feeling place one small penguin-step at a time. Be gentle. Be kind. This doesn't mean that you don't take medicine or have physical therapy or anything of the like. It merely means you do it with a joyful appreciative attitude rather than in an attempt to MAKE the body do something. You are simply showing up with the right mindset.

There are totally healed humans in twisted mangled bodies - because they are happy. Healing is happiness - nothing else. True wealth is an abundance Consciousness even when the purse and account is empty. Real intimate relationship is total love even when there is no other body there. The REAL world has nothing to do with the backward, upside-down, inside-out world that your eyes bear witness to. If you wish to be healed today, simply BE happy and let the physical do whatever the physical does. It has nothing to do with Who and What you are.

25. Work With Us

"For the memory of God can dawn only in a mind that chooses to remember, and that has relinquished the insane desire to control reality. You who cannot even control yourself should hardly aspire to control the universe." -A Course In Miracles

WHILE IT IS SO that the physical world that you see is rooted in attack, defense, survival and competition, you

MUST remember that the <u>Universe</u> is a friendly and cooperative place - and that place is a state of Consciousness. Everywhere that you walk is holy ground and a safe place when you are in that Consciousness, regardless of how the winds of change may blow through the world around you.

Your fear-based desire to manipulate and control the conditions around you is endless, hopeless and extremely draining. Even all of your mental "efforting" in which you are trying to figure it all out is quite debilitating and is based on judging according to appearances. "*Survival of the fittest*" is yet another ego theory which the ego world embraced . . . and it is simply not so. The Universe is based on cooperation, not competition. Competition is based on the scarcity "principle" and it engenders nothing but fear and suffering. Even the "games" you play are based on this principle. You tend to get very excited about things which keep you on the wheel of suffering. This is so strange to Us.

Remember, any solution which the Holy Spirit brings is one in which everyone wins and no one loses. In the ego's philosophy, you are always working ON things rather than working WITH them. Do you see the difference? When you are working ON something, you are stuck in the control mode. It is also rooted in separation. You are SEPARATE from the thing you are working ON - and so often you feel totally alone. It is the model of a mechanistic universe in which you are endlessly tinkering with dead things outside of you. But this is a COOPERATIVE LIVING Universe based on sharing and mutual benefit. <u>Everything is ALIVE with Divine Intelligence</u>! Work WITH that Intelligence dear Miracle Worker!

So often you are working on the relationship, working on your finances, working on the project, working on your weight or health, working on your personality. This is exhausting and hopeless. ALL of these "things" are ALIVE with Divine Intelligence which you could be working in cooperation WITH today. When you are working WITH or playing WITH the relationship, it becomes a living breathing entity rather than a dead mechanistic "thing" which you are trying to manipulate into some predetermined model of what you think it is "supposed" to be. How sad and exhausting to always be trying to FORCE things into a predetermined model of "success." How dull and lonely that path can be.

When Master Teacher Jesus said, *"you must become as little children"* this is one of the things He was teaching. Children see a magical cooperative Universe in which anything and everything can spring to life, from a garden to a tin soldier to a stuffed animal. It's call IMAGINATION and everyone uses it from day one on Earth to the very end - but children use it to call forth the world they want to see, whereas you adults tend to use it to "worry" by calling forth in imagination the things you do NOT want to see. This is mental malpractice.

AWAKEN to the cooperative Universe today Dear One! Work WITH Us today as you work WITH the circumstances of your life. Life will bend TOWARD you today as you make friends with everything in your life and see it not outside yourself but as part of your own Consciousness. DO NOT judge according to appearances, but instead be a teachable cooperative player in your own life rather than the overwhelmed and stressed out micro-manager of a resistant world. Life LOVES you. Cooperate with Life by letting in the love today!

26. Revelation and Miracles

"Revelation unites you directly with God. Miracles unite you directly with your brother. Neither emanates from consciousness, but both are experienced there. Consciousness is the state that induces action, though it does not inspire it. You are free to believe what you choose, and what you do attests to what you believe." -A Course In Miracles

IT IS UNNECESSARY TO ASK GOD FOR A MIRACLE when YOU are the one who is in charge of the miraculous. Do not ask God to do your job for you - it is a waste of time. Remember, miracles are a means of SAVING time. Miracles are in no way supernatural or the exceptions to the laws of the Universe. In fact, they are normal, natural, healing, restorative and common. A miracle is union - nothing more or less. They remind you of your natural state of being and of your relationship to all of Life.

Miracles are what occur between the children of God, not between God and Child. Revelation is what happens between the Divine Parent and you, the Created Ones. Your Divine Parent "reveals" to you through revelation. Think less of a "burning bush" and more in terms of the "still small Voice" within you. Revelation can come from a bumper sticker, a daydream, a book falling from a shelf, or a sudden insight or realization. Do not limit revelation to old-school "religious" imagery, though they may come in that way as well.

Miracles are the realm of the Children of God. When you "ask" for a miracle, please know that you are asking YOURSELF. Getting your rent paid or healing a tumor is NOT a miracle in any way whatsoever. However, those things MAY be the RESULT of a miracle. The real miracle is the internal shift that takes place in the mind of the Miracle

Worker. It is the relinquishment of projecting fear and guilt, and instead focusing on innocence and peace even if you do not realize that is what you are doing. THAT is the miracle - anything that happens in the physical realm after that is merely the RESULT of the miracle.

Therefore, if you really want Divine Aid, ASK instead for a REVELATION of Truth about whatever is in front of you. The purpose of revelation is to aid you in dropping the story which is preventing you from experiencing the transcendent peace of Oneness. The revelation can pave the way; making it much easier for YOU to then DO the miracle you are perfectly capable of doing. Therefore, instead of saying, *"God I need a miracle,"* which is really you being irresponsible for your own vibration, you say,

> *"God of my Being, I need a REVELATION! Reveal to me the Truth. I am ready to drop all my evidence and SEE with Spiritual Vision rather than physical sight. Show me - I want to see!"*

Then, get ready to have your heart opened and your mind blown.

27. Consider These Things

"Wait patiently for Him. He will be there. The light has come. You have forgiven the world . . . from this time forth you will see differently. Today the light has come." -A Course In Miracles

PATIENT, PATIENCE, PATIENTLY . . . We know how you resist and even sometimes hate these words. Yet much of your peace is found in these very words. We understand, patience is difficult because you have trained your minds to be active and even frantic as a sign of intelligence and a superior edge in making things happen. You have no idea how foolish, reversed and ridiculous this is to Us. It is the opposite of Truth.

In fact, most of you tend to think that when a person is quiet, calm, methodical and slow moving that they are somewhat stupid, lazy and idiotic. Once again, you judge by appearances and are easily fooled by a culture and a world designed to chew you up and spit you out. Most humans are complicit in their own murder at the hands of the ego thought system.

Remember that YOU are in charge of your emotional journey each day. YOU choose the thoughts you will think and the concepts that you will believe. You can think thoughts that terrify and abuse you - or you can choose the thoughts that soothe and uplift you.

The Truth is, there is love all around you already. The Light has come and your task is merely to focus your attention on it. You cannot out-give God. You cannot out-love the Universe. But you can get so worried, frantic, busy and preoccupied that you fail to SEE what is right in front of you. Remember that there can be a HUGE difference between being busy and being fruitful. Your command is to be FRUITFUL - you were not told to get busy!

A quiet, focused, open spacious mind is a very fruitful place. Wait for a Word from Source - even ONE Word vibrates with immense healing and Light. You can do it at any moment under any circumstances. You do not need a robe, incense, flowers or candles in a dark quiet room. You can seek His Word in screeching freeway traffic. It is a matter of surrender and willingness to ASK. And through that little crack of willingness, the Light enters and peace is restored.

YOUR resistance only delays the Divine-Timing - and often rushing forward and crashing through barriers is the very worst kind of resistance. We are asking you to SAVOR the waiting time. ENJOY the in-between times because most of your life is spent in these "in-between" times - the times between "peak experiences" and major events. Consider being less busy and more fruitful. Consider the lilies of the field. Consider the birds of the air.

28. Focus Pocus

"To be in the Kingdom is merely to focus your full attention on it." -A Course In Miracles

YOU ARE GETTING MORE of whatever you are focusing on – and focus is vibration. It's really not so much what you are thinking about but rather HOW you are thinking about it that kicks Law into motion. For instance, you may be doing prosperity affirmations everyday, but if you are doing them from a consciousness of scarcity and lack, you are vibrating scarcity and lack. This means that no matter how much money you do or do not have, you will FEEL fearful and depleted.

You focus far too much on the form of things when it is actually the content that has the most impact on you. This modern phenomenon of hoarding and storage units is proof that the accumulation of objects only increases the feeling of emptiness when the mind believes in lack. Even your "homeless" people often push shopping carts full of meaningless garbage which is their "treasure" and part of their self-identification.

Remember, all the things of this world are neutral - even bodies and relationships are neutral. What gives everything meaning is mind. Mind projects and endows meaning. Therefore, BE CONSCIOUS of what meaning you are projecting and FOCUS on content rather than on form. Form is always in a state of the cycling of birth, death and rebirth. Forms are not stable.

The way of the Urban Mystic Miracle Worker is to invoke and infuse. Call forth the very best which is within all life forms by focusing your attention on what is good and true and lovely. Infuse all that you do with the energies of love, joy, peace and kindness. You will find that the magical qualities of your life begin to quicken as everything lines up with your positive focus. People will wonder how you are always at the right place at the right time - how you always get first class treatment - how things seem to "fall in your lap" - how opportunities seem to arise from "out of nowhere" - how problems seem to solve themselves while you are busy napping. And you will tell them that there is no real magic here, no hocus-pocus - YOU have learned the power of something mystical and yet very real that we call FOCUS POCUS.

29. Once Upon A Time

"The Holy Spirit will help you reinterpret everything that you perceive as fearful, and teach you that only what is loving is true." -A Course In Miracles

THERE IS A VOICE NARRATING THE STORY OF YOUR LIFE all day long. It is this voice which determines how you will FEEL about your day, your week, your year, and your life. When you allow the ego to do the voiceover work in the documentary that you call your life, you have relinquished control to an insane producer and director. Therefore, it is important to remember that you have a CHOICE about who will narrate your movie today.

When the ego narrates your story, the sadness, anxiety, excitement, longing, desire, desperation and anger get milked to the very last drop of drama and despair. Overacting is the norm and most anything can become ridiculously intense. Every scene gets played to the balcony for maximum effect and the scenery is being chewed all day long, even if it is all happening mentally while the body remains seemingly calm and normal. This is quite often an inner performance or one done for very private audiences of one or two. At various points, you as the lead character will most likely fall to your knees at the center of the stage and sob something like, *"WHY is this happening or me?"* or *"When is it going to be MY turn?"* Or if you are more of a movie performer, you may become very quiet and still quiet while the camera zooms in for your close-up as you whisper your lines and a single tear very slowly travels down your cheek. It IS a very juicy scene . . . but it makes you FEEL exhausted, depleted and tragically "special."

The Holy Spirit narrates the exact same story and circumstances quite differently. The Holy Spirit is a loving kind and joyous director and producer. The narration is done with love and gentle humor. Under His direction you play the scenes quite differently - some lines get cut and other lines are played up - you find yourself, even in the midst of great loss, saying things like, *"It was so wonderful while it lasted and I will always treasure that time we had together. It made my life so much sweeter."* And you will feel blessed as you smile through the tears. Even the musical score is very different. Everything contributes to the overall FEEL of each scene.

You are always free to tell the story of your day by going one direction or the other. There really is no in-between place. You are either choosing the loving direction of the Holy Spirit, or the fearful path of the ego - and you can tell by how you FEEL, which path you have chosen in that moment.

And the wonderful news is that you can change your mind at ANY MOMENT, no matter how far down the path you have gone. At any second you can fire the ego and begin again with the Holy Spirit. At times you may have to do this over and over again in just one day if an old painful way of thinking has gotten activated. <u>Do not let this discourage you. Be diligent but gentle.</u> Keep choosing the path that activated the Christ Consciousness within you and each small step forward will bring more conviction and more breathing space.

You are not alone. No one is alone. We are here. We are ready. We are listening. All loss is temporary. There is so much more good to come.

30. Sleeping Around

"The mind is very powerful, and never loses its creative force. It never sleeps. Every instant it is creating." -A Course In Miracles

WE WANT TO ASK WHO YOU'VE BEEN SLEEPING WITH lately. And we also want to ask what you've been sleeping with. It is good to be extremely selective in this area, for far too often you have allowed into your bed those who have tormented you all night long. You need to be much more assertive in throwing out those who are not making your nights sweeter and more gloriously restful and renewing. Yes, often it is not so much a case of who you are sleeping with as it is whom you are tossing and turning with all night long. And though it is only in your mind, they often are MORE present with you than the body of a person who IS physically there next to you.

We watch so many of you bring into your bed the co-worker whom you have grievances with, the political leader whom frightens you, the financial situation that is out of your control, the friends of your son who are living a life you do not approve of, the uncertain future of this or that, the mother who is starting to show signs of decline . . . it goes on an on.

PROGRAM YOUR MIND

Disinviting those who are not helping you sleep is very important, but as with ALL the tools we give you, being proactive from the start is a much better way to live. Because of this it is much better to spend some time as you are getting ready to drift off to sleep consciously setting the tone for your slumber. Just who and what are you inviting into your bed? Remember that **the time when you are drifting off to sleep is the very BEST time to begin programming your subconscious mind with positive, soothing and uplifting thoughts.** It already uses that time to do tremendous healing work on your body. This is the ideal time to give it a job to do while you retreat to the Higher Realms in which We download new programs and miracle mindsets to you.

Perhaps you have seen a "dead" body in a casket and heard people say, *"Oh, he looks so peaceful."* Of course, because there is no one in there tormenting the body anymore! We suggest that you stop tormenting your body with your thoughts as well, but there is no need to "die" in order for that to happen. It happens by gently programming the mind to move in a positive direction. The time just before sleep is a POWERFUL time to do so. You may listen to recordings that soothe you to sleep or you could memorize or read some affirmations each night just before bed. Brother Jacob has a wonderful "bedtime prayer" in his book "Invocations" which you could use if you don't already have one.

As you become more diligent about who you are sleeping with each night, you will find that you wake in the morning delighted to see a new day, with gratitude and optimism vibrating through your mind - not immediately, but with consistent practice. It is all cumulative and it all will make a wonderful positive difference. Start where you are. Start today.

31. Something More

"There is nothing about me that you cannot attain. I have nothing that does not come from God. The difference between us now is that I have nothing else. This leaves me in a state which is only potential in you." -A Course In Miracles

PERHAPS YOU HAVE NOTICED how quickly the illusion is falling apart in your present time? And the more quickly it falls apart, the more hysterically the ego turns up the public relations machines so that you will not notice. The false gods are falling from their pedestals faster than a new one can be put up.

At the very same time, you can see the rise in religions,

gurus and spiritual communities. In many cases, this is just a more subtle form of the same old illusion. Over and over the human heart, mind and soul yearns for "something more." From this standpoint, each new achievement simply creates the echo of that suspicion that there must me "something more" than this.

THAT is the lie. It is what keeps the search going on endlessly and hopelessly. As usual, the Truth is quite the opposite. The Answer which will finally satisfy you is NOT for something more, but rather for a "something less." It is not a doing, but an undoing. It is not an adding on to, but a subtraction from.

The problem is not anything that you are lacking but rather all of the myths, lies, stressful concepts, theories, requirements and "needs" that you have added on since you arrived here. Don't misunderstand, this is in NO WAY a teaching of the renunciation of the things of this world. The things of this world are neutral - they have no power. Renunciation can often be just another "added on" thing the ego does to try to "fix" what it sees as a wounded insufficient self.

Have children, don't have children. Get married, don't get married. Buy a house, don't buy a house. Have a career, don't have a career. Have a lot of "stuff," have no "stuff" at all. It is ALL THE SAME. It is all neutral. It is all meaningless of itself. It is WHAT MIND DOES WITH IT THAT ENDOWS IT WITH THE QUALITY OF HEAVEN OR HELL. "As a woman thinketh . . . "

This is a highly individualized curriculum in undoing suffering so that what remains is your natural state of inner peace. Little by little We help to unravel the complicated theories you have accepted as your own. Little by little We

Help to undo all of the "doing" of the world so that what is uncovered is a you which has everything God gave you, and nothing else. We move slowly in order to not terrify you, for even the loss of painful illusions is often grieved and mourned by the false self.

So relax and allow the process. When the ego whispers to you that something essential is missing and you feel that yearning for something more, remember that it is yet another lie designed to keep you on the treadmill to nowhere. Relax and release to Him the thing you think you need and We will gently undo yet another layer of bondage and mental chains. Then, should the thing you thought you needed come to you, you will be able to truly enjoy it without attachment or suffering.

32. The Path of Light

"The way is not hard, but it is very different. Yours is the way of pain, of which God knows nothing. Your way is hard indeed, and very lonely. Fear and grief are your guests, and they go with you and abide with you on the way. But the dark journey is not the way of God's Son. Walk in light and do not see the dark companions, for they are not fit companions for the Son of God, who was created of light and in light." - A Course In Miracles

THE WORLD YOU SEE AND BELIEVE IN is the exact opposite of Reality in almost every way imaginable. And you suffer to the extent that you believe in the "rules" of this world of sacrifice, pain, sickness, deprivation and scarcity. You cannot reconcile these two worlds no matter how hard you try. Reconciling the irreconcilable is a waste of your time an energy

- which you could instead be using to savor and enjoy the PRESENT moment exactly as it is and as it is not.

The Prostitute Archetype is strong with the humans. This archetype is not really about sex for money but rather is about how you "sell out" in order to GET what you think you need. The dark companions are like pimps who keep you from the joy of your life by getting you involved in sales and bargaining with your brother. Rather than focusing on the joy of creating and channeling your art, you get focused on trading it for food and money. Rather than focusing on the love given and received in the relationship you tend to focus on the logistics of your "needs" within the relationship, and on making trade-outs to provide a need in exchange for GETTING a need met. This is the primary way the ego sucks the JOY out of your entire life, one incident at a time.

Too often you trust money more than God. You trust medicine more than God. You trust a marriage license more than God. You trust a marketing plan more than God. This makes you sad, lonely and afraid. And the path of the world is one of ever diminishing results. The ego strategies that seemed to work for you in the beginning now bring in less and less results the farther you walk with the dark companions. THIS IS GOOD. It should be the wake-up call that causes you to question that path. Instead, most humans simply double and triple their efforts within this unworkable plan.

Of course the Answer is to ABANDON THIS PATH, ABANDON THIS PLAN. Turn to the Light. Turn within. Come inside and abide with Him. To KNOW God is to dwell with God. Relationship is born from time invested together. The Voice within you will lead you onto the Path of Light and take you on a journey without distance. There is little required other than willingness, willingness, willingness.

Do you want to be happy? Do you want to be free? Do you want a peace the world cannot touch? Do you want true rest? Do you want JOY and laughter and love without limit? All of this the Path of Light offers you each and every day, every moment.

It starts with SURRENDER. Wave the white flag. Call off the search. End the audition. Fire your pimp and give yourself fully to the One Whose only purpose is your perfect happiness. No one is ever rejected. Everyone is accepted. No matter what you have or have not done in the past, you are welcomed home with open arms and gifts.

Begin now. Take a deep breath. Let your shoulders drop. Release your jaw and all the tension in your body. Relax your buttocks and sink down into the chair. Let all anxiety drain out your finger tips and the soles of your feet like sand running through an hourglass. There is nothing to do. Nothing to GET, or fix, or change. There is just YOU, returning to the Great Mother Tao, relaxing into the stream of Golden Light as it carries you effortlessly and gently down the stream. And as you relax, let everything go to the Stream. Give over everything that you have been carrying with you - everything that no longer serves you. And then simply LISTEN for the Voice within. Your Answer for today may not come in words but it will come - perhaps as a feeling, an image, a realization, a Divine Idea.

33. The Widening Gap

"When you come to the place where the branch in the road is quite apparent, you cannot go ahead. You must go either one way or the other. For now if you go straight ahead, the way you went before you reached the

branch, you will go nowhere. The whole purpose of coming this far was to decide which branch you will take now." -A Course In Miracles

A S USUAL, THE EGO'S SLIGHT OF HAND has gotten you distracted by the left hand so that you will not see what the right hand is doing. You are correct that there is an ever-widening gap being created in your physical world, but it is not a gap between the "haves" and the "have-nots." It is not a gap in opportunity and it has nothing to do with worldy conspiracies. It is nothing more or less than a widening gap in Consciousness. The gap is not about money or opportunity - it is a gap between victim fear-based consciousness and Divine Mind Consciousness. There are billionaires who are living in victim consciousness - and many people living simple modest lives who are of Divine Mind Consciousness - and the opposite of both of these is just as true.

The realities are splitting. This is the ending that the Mayan calendar represents. In your particular illusions of time and space, you are fast approaching a collective branching of the road. Remember that you cannot register two different worlds - the vision of one costs you the vision of the other. The splitting of the world is not physical - it is vibrational. Both realities will exist on the same physical plane, but will begin to see and recognize each other less and less.

Those who live in the fear-based consciousness will see much more to be fearful about and will see almost nothing to feel optimistic about. They will be seeing that which is vibrating at the frequency of fear and limitation. Those who are living in Divine Presence Consciousness will find that more and more they are registering only others who find beauty, love, peace, joy and a limitless well of good as their dominant reality.

This is not exclusive of course. Those living in fear

will still see beauty and will notice those who are living in Grace - but they will consider it an anomaly or as part of the great conspiracy against them. Those living in Grace will still experience the ordinary problems and issues of physical existence in the material world, but they will feel Our Presence through it all and they will see the evidence of a Divine Conspiracy for their healing, renewal, promotion and illumination. They will give help to the suffering but will not try to "save" anyone, knowing that only a true shift in perception can save anyone from their own worldview. This is a time to support that which supports the world you choose rather than giving your attention to the world you do not want.

Lean on Us in the coming days, weeks and years dear Mystic - there is already so much good in your life and to the extent that you focus on gratitude and praise to the Creator, you open yourself to an ever expansive Consciousness of allowing your good rather than EARNING and struggling for it. This is a time of LETTING GO rather than holding on. Go in the direction of your joy rather than in the direction of your worldly strategies and limitations. <u>THINK IN TERMS OF JOY rather than in terms of getting and forcing</u>. You may be thinking you'd like to live in London or start your own business - and your ego mind begins trying to figure it all out: *"That looks impossible for me but how can I MAKE that happen and get what I want?"* This is the dark fear-based ego consciousness. It is high-functioning victim consciousness. Remember, victim consciousness often has a "can do" attitude - AND what you work hard to bring into your life you will have to forever work hard to KEEP.

But, the Divine Presence Consciousness says, *"I feel my joy calling me to _____. I am surrendering this process now to Spirit as I start moving in that direction and taking little steps forward with non-attachment. I will daily consult Spirit and seek Divine Guidance as I follow my hunches. I will walk through the open doors and if no doors open, then I know it is not for my highest good and I will stay put unless or until I am lifted by Spirit."*

Don't make life so hard for yourselves. We've got this, but only to the extent that you SURRENDER it to Us! God gives free will and YOU get to choose. And as ever, we remain on ever vigilant standby, ready to respond to your slightest invitation. Now go enjoy your day knowing Who walks beside you.

34. Wisdom Sounds Foolish

""Except ye become as little children" means that unless you fully recognize your complete dependence on God, you cannot know the real power of the Son in his true relationship with the Father. The specialness of God's Son's does not stem from exclusion but from inclusion. All my brothers are special." -A Course in Miracles

IN THE EGO'S WORLD, what passes for conventional wisdom is usually 180 degrees away from the thinking of God. The things emphasized by humans are unseen in the Heavenly State. Your world is quite the opposite of Truth and it is this that causes much of your suffering and stress. The wisdom of the world says "*hold on*" and We say "*let go.*" The world says "*make it happen*" and We say "*get out of the way and let it happen.*" The world says "*I am what my past made of me*" and We say "*your past is just an illusory story you tell yourself.*" The world says "*competition is necessary, good and how you win in life*" and We say "*competition is what has driven your world into fear and despair.*" You make the most simple things extremely complicated and very little scares you as much as looking or feeling naive. The only thing that tends to scare your more than being seen as foolish is not being seen at all.

And yet Brother Jesus said *"Ye must become as little children"* in order to enter the Kingdom. We have told you many times that the Kingdom IS Joy. Little children are joyful because of their thinking, because of their simple faith. It is the simplicity of children which allows them so much access to Joy. You must allow yourself to become much more simple in your faith and belief. And you must release this ridiculous fear of appearing foolish. <u>The Christ always appears foolish to those who are living by ego domination of the flesh</u>. This does not mean that you need go around spouting all your pearls of wisdom to those who do not have ears to hear them. "Marketing" Truth or love or peace or healing is simply more evidence that you believe you need to micromanage the Universe and that Truth needs "help" from you.

<u>We have not lost your file</u>. We know where and how to find you. <u>We know how to best use you and to care for you. We know what you need far better than you ever will or could</u>. We desire your happiness totally, whereas you desire your happiness but are somewhat conflicted about it because of your current beliefs and expectations. When fear arises in you, it is almost always because you have turned from Source to some degree. You are *"too busy"* again, or things were going so well that your ego started to get cocky thinking it was "creating" your reality and all humility flew out the window. And you do not see that the vast majority of your plans are merely defenses against chaos because of the ego's whispering to you that there is no God and that you are truly separate and alone in a dangerous and uncaring world. You find cold comfort in all your strategies and plans for the future.

And yet what a relief it is to you when you finally let go. How often We see that your joy begins with tears - the tears that come when you finally surrender and feel the rush of relief that wells up within you as you release the struggle at last. You spend so much time resisting falling to your knees, and when you finally do it is so magnificent and soul-relieving that you think you will never get back up into that lonely but exciting rat race again. Yet return to it you usually do - not all at once perhaps, but by and by.

Please understand, We have no desire to take away the fun you have from "doing" in the world. We merely want to take away all the anxiety, stress and suffering that comes with it when you think YOU are the doer. We want you to have the joy that children have in doing except with a spiritual maturity and detachment from getting "your way" that children often have. In that sense, you are often still very much a child. So now We are urging you to become as a spiritually mature child - to climb up into the lap of the Mother-Father God and cast your cares upon the Divine Presence. Include God in every single step that you take today and keep that Intimacy immediate and fresh in your Consciousness. Do nothing on your own today - instead, joyfully offer everything over. Make your joy a gift to God as a sign of gratitude for all that has been given, for nothing pleases the Divine Parent more than seeing a happy Child at play.

35. *The Secret Place*

"When we are ready, God Himself will take the final step in our return to Him." -A Course in Miracles

YOUR READINESS simply has to do with doing YOUR part so that God can do God's part. And your part is the guiding of your own mind through your free will faculty. It is YOUR job to make yourself happy each day because happiness has already been given freely by God. But free will allows you to dwell on worry, fear, grudges and grievances and every appearance of limitation if you so choose. This is why the Course in Miracles workbook Helps you to learn to train your mind in the direction of Truth and Light. But even mind training will only take you so far. Remember that Grace cannot be earned through good works or even through mind training. It comes by surrender to It.

At the end of your part is God's part - and that will carry you across the bridge to the Secret Place of the Most High. This is not a journey that you can make yourself in any way. You are carried there as God comes to you. It is a place of mystical Christ Consciousness. You may dwell there even as you go about your normal daily life. It has nothing to do with the death of the body but rather of a kind of death of allegiance to the ego thought system. Oh, you will continue to have ego thoughts, but now you understand them as such rather than taking them personally - and you find your refuge and security in God rather than in your psychology, strategies, plans, defenses and worldly means.

If grief, sorrow, pain, worry or anything threatens your peace of mind, rise up and retreat to the Secret Place of the Most High where you fellowship with the Ascended Masters of Light. There, the Brotherhood and Sisterhood minister to you and work on your Consciousness. Some choose to live the remainder of their physical lives in this Secret Place, all while living what look to be perfectly normal lives on the material realm. From this Place they receive their sustenance and daily bread, while on the Earth plane they continue to guide their own thoughts, choose peace and happiness, be of service, contribute, let go and release all grievances, while giving endless praise and thanksgiving. They do THEIR part and leave the rest to God. It is a very sweet way to live - in the world but not of it.

Whatever confronts you today, you are not alone. Today, focus less on your own thoughts and opinions about what is happening and instead, seek the thoughts of God. Should you find yourself engaged again in the battle with the ego thought system and the appearances of the world, take a moment to step back and let Him lead the way as you rise up to the Secret Place of the Most High. Let today unfold from Consciousness rather than from any strategy you may have to conquer the day. We love to Help you. We love to make the crooked places straight. We love to smooth out the rough spots. Let Us. Invite Us. You are not alone.

36. The Subject of Supply

"In your world you do need things. It is a world of scarcity in which you find yourself because you are lacking . . . As Mediator between the two worlds, He (Holy Spirit) knows what you have need of and what will not hurt you. Ownership is a dangerous concept if it is left to you." -A Course in Miracles

IN YOUR CONTEMPORARY METAPHYSICS, many have made the mistake of thinking of Spirit or God as the Source of your supply. This is precisely the kind of error and misunderstanding that ego loves to make because it has just enough of the ring of Truth to it to keep you just outside the gates of Heaven.

Spirit is not the Source of your supply. <u>Spirit IS supply itself</u>. To think of God as the Source of supply makes of God a bank, a matchmaker, a real estate agent and an errand boy. This leads not to love but rather to the same kind of loyalty that you might have to your local credit union - it is a business arrangement rather than a relationship and it does not give you the peace and comfort that you deserve.

The confusion is in thinking that supply is money, property, health, career, mates and such. But these are the evidence or fruits of supply, not the supply itself. The happy journey is not one that goes in search of the evidence of supply but rather the seeking for True Supply Itself, which is the Presence of God within you. <u>God is the Supply that satisfies and satiates</u>. When you seek for the evidence of supply, what you receive still leaves you in a state in which you will soon be hungry and wanting again. The products, forms and evidence of supply can never give you any lasting sense of security. Only the Presence Itself need be demonstrated in your life. Seek only to demonstrate God rather than demonstrating things. To demonstrate God is to so immerse yourself in the Divine Presence each day that awareness of God is your dominant Consciousness, your dominant energy. In time, it will begin to radiate from you like and invisible radio signal.

If you wish a happiness, peace and Joy that surpasses all understanding, make a 180 degree turn around this very day. Release God as your errand boy and instead begin running errands for God. Surrender everything in your life to the Mother-Father Presence and do it all for God. When you make a bank deposit, remember that it is not your account, but God's. When you bathe and feed your body remember that it is not yours, but rather a loaner that you've been given to use while you are here working for God. When you are cleaning your home, remember that you are not cleaning your home, but are cleaning the place where God is residing. When you make dinner for your family, keep in mind that you are preparing food for those whom God has sent into your life to be helped by you and see it as a great honor that you are NOT doing for them but for God.

And do NOT make the mistake of seeing this as some serious religious mission but rather as a JOYFUL temp job that you have the pleasure of doing while you reside here in this world. <u>Bring laughter, lightness and FUN to all of your doings as best you can</u>. Spirit wants to experience JOY and fun THROUGH YOU. Being used by Spirit is the MOST joyful way to live when it is understood correctly and not usurped by the ego's religions. We have need of YOU, not another bland self-sacrificing religious type who is so good that she is good for nothing. Bring ALL of you to the job and We will not only make wonderful joyous use of you, but will provide all the evidence of supply that will be most helpful to you and the job you came to do.

37. Perceiving the Body

"The body is in need of no defense. This cannot be too often emphasized. It will be strong and healthy if the mind does not abuse it by assigning it to roles it cannot fill, to purposes beyond its scope, and to exalted aims which it cannot accomplish. Such attempts, ridiculous yet deeply cherished, are the sources for the many mad attacks you make upon it. For it seems to fail your hopes, your needs, your values and your dreams." -A Course in Miracles

IT IS THE ENDLESS OBSESSION WITH THE BODY and identification with it that causes so many of your perceived physical problems. And the more focus you have on the body, the worse it tends to get in your perception. Fight and "conquer" one condition here, and another one pops up over there. Take care of that one, and now another one has shown up in a different area. Because of this body obsession you fear food, germs, sex, the air, water, your genetics . . . it really is endless, exhausting and hopeless. And surely you must know by now that you create what you defend against. What you push against, grows stronger and more virulent. Your "fitness" industry has created rampant obesity by pushing against, pushing against, pushing against.

Give your body to Us and end your obsession with it! Turn it over so that it may be used for a Divine Purpose - communication. That is all the Holy Spirit sees the body as for - a means of communication to the rest of the Sonship. It has no other purpose and does not need all your endless defenses nor purification cleansing rites. It is neither sinful nor good. It is wholly neutral. Turn it over to the Higher Authority and let it be used by Us as you turn your attention to what matters most - your thoughts. Other than that, use common sense.

Remember, this is a HIGHLY INDIVIDUALIZED curriculum. Each body seeks its own balance and will find it through Us if you will stop your worry and obsession with it. The foods, movements, treatments, even physicians and healers that are perfect for YOUR particular body is different than it is for your neighbor. Nutrition and exercise trends have been going on since the days of the cavemen and don't amount to much. The body is an expression of Consciousness. Offer it to the Christ Consciousness ONLY. Then you will begin to eat with JOY, move with JOY, express sexually (or not) with JOY.

And yes, your body will go through changes. Bodies are not meant to last forever. They are merely part of the Earth Temp Assignment you took on. They will show signs of age and the shape and size will change as you go. Change is natural. It is not to be seen as another enemy to wage war with nor is it a barometer of your Consciousness. The body is an EXPRESSION of Consciousness, not a chart. Many of your "enlightened" masters had chronic physical conditions and many ego-driven serial killers have vibrantly healthy bodies. The bodily EXPRESSION of Consciousness has to do with how you PERCEIVE the body at any given time.

So what is the proper way to look at the body? WITH KINDNESS ONLY. It is not something to be conquered, regimented, punished, used to attract, whipped into shape, hated, avoided, denied, feared or abused. It is to be thought of and treated with kindness and non-attachment. For now, use this question as your guide in regards to the body, *"Is this kind?"* You know that when you are eating large amounts of food until you feel stuffed and bloated that that does not feel like kindness. You know that when you are denying yourself all pleasure in eating that that does not feel kind. You know when your thoughts and actions feel kind or if they stem from deprivation or over-indulgence. Seek the balance of KINDNESS and turn over your body to the Christ Consciousness each time you think of it today. Then, do it again tomorrow and the next day. Make of it a habit. And when you need help with it, ASK Us to guide you to all the right resources and Help. We are here for you - make good use of Us.

38. The Everlasting Arms

"The holy relationship reflects the true relationship the Son of God has with the Father in reality . . . Here is the way to true relationships held gently open, through which you and your brother walk together, leaving the body thankfully behind and resting in the Everlasting Arms. Love's Arms are open to receive you, and give you peace forever." -A Course in Miracles

REST IN THE EVERLASTING ARMS TODAY little Miracle Worker. This is a rest and a peace that the world cannot give and that refreshes as no sleep ever has or could. It is the rest that comes from lack of worry and from a trust in the Source of Life Itself to carry you through the day no matter what comes.

Of yourself, you can never create or find the strength and security that this relationship gives you. Of yourself, you could never arrange life to be free of all stress and worry. But as you rest in the Everlasting Arms of the Christ Consciousness and sense your Oneness with the great Mother-Father Creator, you find that you have within you all that you need regardless of what the day brings. To the extent that you focus on this ONE relationship, all other relationships begin to fall in line through the power of Grace - work relationships, friendships, family, community relationships all begin to go through a miraculous process when you stop focusing on what to DO about these relationships and instead surrender them all to God as YOU rest in the Everlasting Arms.

You may give yourself fully to the Everlasting Arms today even in the midst of a very busy day. Consciousness must be conscious OF something in order to be consciousness. Today, be Conscious of the Presence of the

Arms of God surrounding you and holding you gently in tender fierce Love as you calmly and joyfully walk through your day knowing that wherever you are, GOD IS, and all is well.

39. A Brilliant Future

"I place the future in the hands of God." -A Course in Miracles

IN YOUR PARTICULAR CULTURE, the vast majority of suffering comes not from some kind of physical bondage or tyranny, but rather from an internal mental bondage and tyranny. It is the battlefield of the mind on which most of your wars are raging. And many of the wars which torment you the most have to do with an illusory imaginary future as you try to manipulate and control it out of fear of WHAT MIGHT HAPPEN!!!

But with right thinking today, tomorrow takes care of itself. There is no future, only the ever-present now stretching out into eternity and beyond. What you are thinking today will most likely be what you are thinking tomorrow. These are mental habit patterns that continue on unless they are guided and changed. If you love what you are thinking and it feels good - how delightful, continue on. However, if you do NOT love or like what you are thinking and it feels stressful, you would be wise to begin guiding your thoughts in a different direction.

So, when it comes to the future, His Course reminds you to *"place the future in the hands of God"* if you must believe in a future. Remember that *"lots can happen"* when it comes to possibilities for your greater good, and you do not have to know HOW it will all happen. Your ego mind will always see limited finite possibilities for your future good because it thrives in a world of scarcity. In fact, We joke that the ego is the mayor of "Scare City."

But miracle worker, YOU live in the City of Light, which is set on a hill. You are not under the ridiculous laws of the illusory world, nor are you limited to its finite resources. YOU walk in the Grace and favor of God, IF you choose to focus your attention and Consciousness there. Free will allows you to register and focus on whichever world you choose.

Today you can place the future in the hands of God and focus on thinking thoughts that feel good in your PRESENT. <u>The future is born from the present and what you think today is forming your tomorrows</u>. Join with Us in thinking thoughts that soothe and uplift as you release the idea that there is a future that needs defending and strategizing. Yes, there will be plans to make but they are not "*self-initiated*" plans in which you are trying to "*cover your ass*" and control what cannot be controlled. You WILL make gentle plans that come from wisdom within and if they change along the way, you will not be attached. As you lean on God, more and more you will trust that all things are held perfectly in the hands of God - because that is where YOU put them.

<u>Expect things to go well. Expect your day to unfold in perfect order and beauty. Expect Divine Aid and to be greeted by Angels on every corner</u>. Expect the crooked place to be made straight as you continue to detach from specific outcomes. We have a glorious day of love and joy planned if you will only join Us in the Divine Will rather than trying to get Us to join in your will. Remember, a bright and brilliant future is the child of the bright and brilliant thoughts of today.

40. Heading For the Pole

"Where the mind goes, the man follows." –Anonymous

THERE IS A STORY TOLD of a long stretch of road in the desert leading from California to Las Vegas where there is a tendency for drivers to fall asleep at the wheel and crash into electrical poles. Considering the distance between these poles you would think that the chances of hitting the poles rather than simply driving off the road would be rather low - yet the opposite is true. MANY drive right into those poles as if they were the goal.

What tends to occur is that as the speeding driver goes off the road and starts hitting bumps, he awakens, grabs the wheel and focuses all of his attention on NOT HITTING THE POLE ahead of him. Consequently he usually plows right into the pole. <u>Awareness is such that where the mind goes, the body follows</u>. If your attention is on AVOIDING something, you are most likely headed exactly in that direction.

This is another great misunderstanding of the *"law of attraction"* because you tend to think of it in terms of what you are *"attracting to you"* when in fact the law has much more to do with WHAT YOU ARE ATTRACTED TO. And you are attracted to whatever your attention is on, even if you HATE what you are focused on. In fact, you are heading right for it. Where the mind goes, the body follows. Job said, *"The thing I have greatly feared has come upon me"* - because he was heading right for it by keeping it active in his consciousness as he *"greatly feared"* it. <u>It's not about what you attract, but what you are attracted TO that has the most impact in your life</u>. Hate your fat and watch it grow. Hate your creditors and watch your debt grow. Hate your disease and watch it thrive. <u>Your</u>

attention is your attraction TO IT, not its attraction to you.

Where your mind goes, the body will follow sooner or later. Keep your mind on the direction that you want to be traveling in. Start heading for the joy, the peace, the prosperity, the love, the kindness, the wholeness, the healing, the good . . . even if everyone else is running around like Chicken Little declaring that the sky is surely falling. There is nothing to avoid, only something to move toward. CHOOSE now what you are moving toward so that your great quote will be *"what I have greatly loved has come upon me."*

When you begin to *"greatly fear"* anything simply remind yourself, *"Uh oh, I'm heading for the pole. The pole is not after me. It cannot come and get me. I am the one heading for the pole through my attention to it. And so, I'm changing direction right now and heading for the smooth open road."*

41. The Tree of Life

"The grass is pushing through the soil, the trees are budding now, and birds have come to live within their branches. Earth is being born again in new perspective. Night has gone, and we have come together in the light."
–A Course in Miracles

GOD THE CAUSE, YOU THE EFFECT. This is the paradigm which will give you the peace and freedom that you deserve. When you make anything but the Divine Presence a cause in your life, you suffer. Fruit is an effect. Health, money, companionship, happiness, success . . . these are all fruits, they are all effects. But humans tend to make them causes. If you believe that what was done to you as a child is a cause in your life, then you have made of your childhood an idol which has replaced God - and you will not be able to fully experience the peace and joy of God that is seeded within you. If you make the economy, the job market, your marriage or lack of one, if you make any of these a cause in your life, you are living in a house made of cards.

Look not to the fruit but to that Life that causes the Fruitage to come forth. Focus your attention and loving-kindness on the Tree rather than on the fruit and though the seasons will change, you will not be afraid when you go through the winters. Tend to the Tree of Life with consistency. This is what your prayer and meditation is - tending to the ONE Relationship from which all others flow. In your relationship with the One, all other relationships begin to be the fruit of THAT relationship. Through the relationship with the Tree of Life you receive wisdom and understanding that carries you through all the seasons. You will not panic when the tide goes out, when the sun goes down, when the tree is barren. You will understand the natural rising and falling of effects as you learn to focus your attention on the One Cause from which only good flows. All other causes are lesser and will give you a somewhat mixed bag of illusions, both wanted and unwanted.

God the Cause. You the effect. A formula for lasting peace and happiness.

42. Be Careful What You Are Activating

"What would the feeling be like if it were true that you are what you want to be? That they are what they want to be? That they have what they want? Don't ask how it is going to happen, the depth of your own being has ways and means your conscious surface being knows not of, but it will

happen." -Neville Goddard

THE BETTER IT GETS, THE BETTER IT GETS. The worse it gets, the worse it gets. When it rains, it pours. Them that's got shall get, them that's not, shall lose. You humans have many pithy little sayings of truth to remind you . . . yet, you keep right on forgetting that whatever direction you are headed in is taking you to more of the same when it comes to your attitudes, awareness and perceptions.

As We often like to remind you, if every time you voiced a negative or fear-based thought a tooth fell out, most of you would need to have broth for dinner tonight because you'd have nothing to chew with by the end of day one. Of course, many of you don't even think you are speaking negativity and fear - you feel you are simply *"telling it like it is"* and reporting the *"facts"* as if the world had asked you for some kind of press release.

We want to remind you that *"telling it like it is"* simply brings more of what is. As one teacher so wisely stated, better to be emotionally biased than historically accurate. In other words, speak the words that FEEL good - be emotionally biased by telling stories that feel good simply BECAUSE they feel good. We are not talking about a fearful negative suppression of things, because that is just another kind of focusing on what is unwanted. Pushing something down actually gives it your attention.

What we are saying is that if something is happening that strikes fear in your heart and mind, bring it to the Altar within and surrender to Us your thoughts and perceptions of it. From that point on, walk in the faith and knowledge that you are being guided and directed in all ways concerning the issue. Once again, Our greeting to you is, *"Fear not! Be not afraid!"* This is the precursor to most every miracle that has ever happened. Activate the Miracle Principle today by carefully choosing the words you speak and the thoughts you will entertain.

43. So What?

"We are not going to put up a "wall" against illness. Instead, our response will be: What about it? Is it power? Is it a presence? Is it reality? Or is all power the consciousness of the individual, which is the law of health? And this growth, this pain, or this lack, is it law? No, of course, it is not." -Joel Goldsmith

HUMANS TEND TO BE EXPERTS in all the wrong things and your interest is often in whatever frightens you the most. Your internet is often used as a tool to first terrify yourselves with "information", and then as a kind of protection and defense against possible catastrophe, or to feed an insatiable thirst for the kind of knowledge that does not truly help or uplift you as beings. The study of error is the great pastime of the ego-dominated thought system. If only you were as interested in studying the nature of Infinite Spirit you would soon find that the vast majority of your "problems" would simply vanish like dew off the grass under the warming rays of the summer morning sun.

You must let go of rehearsing your fears and memorizing new "facts" to terrify yourself with each day. Instead, begin to become mesmerized by the Divine Presence within all things. As you do this you can arrive at the place where your response to words like cancer, aids, divorce, catastrophe, theft and yes, even death, will be a simple and quiet but firm *"so what?"* NOT that you would say this out loud to another human, but that within your own Consciousness you could go directly to your knowledge and awareness of Who and What God is rather than focusing on the who and what of the human storyline. This Consciousness is what you lean on and turn to rather than wasting energy FIGHTING against some condition. In this Consciousness you can still take medicine, respond to a law suit, file a police report, make the appointment or do whatever is the next logical step in "action" terms - but you do it FROM a Consciousness of thinking or saying:

> *"I have consulted a Higher*
> *Authority and It has the Answer to*
> *any problem or condition that*
> *comes my way today."*

Too often humans waste precious energy in telling the world and God about how big your problems are rather than telling your problems how HUGE your God is. As usual, the ego mind has everything exactly reversed from what Reality is and all priorities are in opposite order of importance. Very little is as outrageous to an individual ego than to try to take away their role of "victim" in their personal story. You would think that humans would be THRILLED to throw off such a debilitating and cruel self-perception and yet there nothing that it clings to more than this.

But not you dear Light Worker! You are here with Us now and you keep on choosing a Higher Authority. You are doing an excellent job - now, keep going. Do not stop. Each day a penguin step forward - no racing and no competition necessary - just a nice steady gait will do the trick.

If anything threatens your peace of mind today, let

your first response within be, *"So what? Do you have any idea Who I work for, Who my God is, what is possible in this Divine Presence? You have no power here at all. Be gone before someone drops a house on you!"* And then take a deep breath and walk on in the illumination of Divine Awareness, all the while reminding yourself of all the attributes of God and of all the miracles that you have already witnessed and of all the miracles that have come down through human history. STUDY this and rehearse this 10 times more than each illness and problem that you study and you will become an expert in the peace that passes all understanding. If you want to search the internet today, let it be for words like *"miracle, inner peace, serenity, kindness . . .* maybe even *"kittens.""*

44. Time For Review

"You are much too tolerant of mind wandering, and are passively condoning your mind's miscreations." -A Course in Miracles

SOME OF YOU HAVE ALLOWED THE EGO TO STEAL at least some of your joy again as you've become a bit sloppy and lazy about your vibration. You don't even realize how many of your thoughts and conversations are at least mild whining, complaining, self-pitying, blaming, grumbling, murmuring, faultfinding, rehearsing your fears, worrying, talking lack, speaking limitation, giving voice to problems and so on. And you need to accept the fact that it really does not matter how "legitimate" or good your reasons for this are - you are only hurting yourself. You may call it "venting" or "clearing" but it is detrimental to your happiness unless you are doing it in the context of KNOWING that it is all a bunch of crap and you are saying it to someone who doesn't believe a word of it but who is listening kindly without judgment for a BRIEF period, and certainly no more than once a week.

You must NOT indulge the ego unless you are deeply questioning what it tells you. This is what the 4 questions of "the work" and the worksheets are for, remember? Knowledge is only POTENTIAL power. You must USE the tools and what you know in order for them to have an effect.

No one else is doing this to you even though you may have a lot of evidence that they are. It has merely become the excuse you use for cutting yourself off from your own connection to the Divine Presence within you and your own JOY. This is not the advice We would give the general public, but for you Graduate Student Practitioners, it is IMPERATIVE that you remember these Truths.

<u>This is the time for you to free the hostages once again</u>! It is time to turn this energy pattern around - to make a better choice. You must NOT be passive in this. <u>YOU are responsible for what you think and what you say</u> - and all those thoughts and words manifest instantly into "thought forms" which ARE your current reality of the moment even if they never manifest physically.

The reality you are creating IS in form - thought forms. And your thought forms are far more real to you than any "physical" thing that you experience. Again, you are far too focused on physical form when it is THOUGHT FORM that has the greatest impact on your moment-to-moment daily life. THINK ABOUT WHAT YOU ARE THINKING ABOUT and CHOOSE the thoughts, attitudes and words that massage you to a better and better feeling place. A though form is a "thing" and ALL things have a gravitational pull. Therefore, every thought is PULLING toward it whatever matches that thought vibration.

In particular, as you enter the increased cultural vibrational frequencies at various times of the year (holidays and such) it is very important to take your own emotional journey and not look to other people and situations to give you the feeling you want to have. YOU are responsible for your own happiness and this is the best news of all! The world, God, your family, the economy, a spouse, a career, having a certain kind of body, children, money or worldly success - none of these have been assigned to you to make you happy. That is YOUR job.

And if you find that "they" are frustrating and upsetting you - go right ahead and judge the crap out of them in your own mind. Think all the ego thoughts that you can muster about them - and at the end of it all say, "*just like me.*" Then, once again realize that life is simply a mirror showing you your own beautiful and horrifying self over and over again. At this point it is much easier to release the hostages and to release yourself as you start over again. Perhaps you have not fallen entirely into the ditch but are gently and ever-so-slightly starting to veer off into minor frustration or slight melancholy or something that seems like "no big deal" - well, NIP IT IN THE BUD RIGHT NOW. <u>Ego loves to GRADUALLY lure you into hell rather than hurl you in all at once</u>. Make a DECISION NOW to turn entirely toward the Light again and get back on track. We think you are doing an amazing job and We love how you get yourself back to JOY.

45. *Contagious Moods & Attitudes*

"If you don't take care of yourself, don't worry, someone else will - in

THEIR way." –Reverend Terry

IF YOU DO NOT TAKE RESPONSIBILITY for managing your own moods and attitudes, the world will, in IT'S way. And as you already are well aware, the moods and attitudes of the world tend sharply toward the negative and fearful. Moods and attitudes are not only a matter of individual humans, entire countries can fall under a dark mood or attitude if enough of the people living within have that Consciousness.

BUT, the Miracle Worker is NOT one who is tossed about as a victim living at the effect of the attitudes of those she is surrounded by! NO! She takes responsibility for A STEELY DETERMINATION TO FOCUS ONLY ON THE POSITIVE ASPECTS OF LIFE as she amps up the vibrations of gratitude and appreciation within herself. She is not trying to convince anyone else. She is not hiding at home away from all the "negative" people. She is not trying to create a world in which she will be more comfortable. SHE IS TAKING HER OWN EMOTIONAL JOURNEY TO JOY by each thought that she thinks and each word that she speaks.

The Urban Mystic is not keeping watch and record of where people are getting it wrong, but rather is noticing where they are getting it right. He is not focusing on their differences and separation, but on their similarities and union. He is not going around trying to "*cheer people up*" and get them to become more "*positive*" but is instead radiating his own Christic Joy without attachment to what others are doing or saying, knowing that his own mood and attitude is also contagious to those who are susceptible. This attitude is a magnet to those who are also focusing their attention on the positive aspects of life.

During the holidays seasons you may be thrown together with people whom you do not agree with, who seem very far from where you are vibrationally, who do not share the same attitudes that you do, who are not doing things your way - and your ego will tempt you to discard them, throw them away, cut them off, focus on their "wrongness" and limitations or to try to recruit them to your way of seeing and doing life. DO NOT ALLOW THIS TO HAPPEN TO YOU! Instead, become radically defenseless and open. Simply refuse to take anything personally. You may think quietly to yourself,

> *"Good for them, that's what they are up to and I have no idea what anyone's perfect path is. That has nothing to do with me. I am staying in my own yard, cleaning up my own Consciousness. If they want my help or opinion, they'll ask for it. And even if they ask and then refute it, good for them, that has nothing to do with me! I think I'll try to find something wonderful about them and focus entirely on that."*

The truth is, people are much more open to your mood and attitude if they see that you are coming from a place of internal peace and non-attachment - that you are not trying to change them or sell them on anything. People do not want to be fixed, they want to be loved and accepted just as they are - because it is transformative to be loved and accepted.

So again, CHOOSE your daily mood and attitude first thing every morning. Do NOT wait to see what happens first and <u>DO NOT LET THE EGO STEAL YOUR JOY</u> because of something that someone else says or does, or fails to say or do. <u>RELEASE THE HOSTAGES</u> and keep massaging your own thoughts to the better feeling place by amping up your attention on the positive aspects of anything and everything around you - even if you have to go so far as to say to yourself, *"You know, the GREAT thing about this problem is _____."*

And should you find that all your plans fall through and you are in a situation which tempts you to tell yourself a stressful and sad story about what is happening - once again take charge of your mood and attitude. Admit that you do not like what is happening, let it out, and then CHOOSE how you want to FEEL in spite of what is happening and get back on the highlighted route to inner peace.

It is YOUR consistency that defeats the ego in its attempts at stealing your joy. And remember to ask the Holy Spirit for Help - <u>don't just think about prayer, PRAY</u>! We know that this has the potential to be the most enjoyable miraculous holiday season you have experienced so far - no matter what happens.

46. A Culture of "Size Matters"

"Do not despise the days of small beginnings, for the LORD rejoices to see the work begin . . ." -Zeckariah 4:10

"*D*REAM BIG!" "Go big or go home!! Life your BEST life! You can have it ALL!" Maximum, huge, super-size, quantum, plus, double bonus . . . the words of your world tend toward the philosophy that more is the key to happiness and that it is the ultimate sign of "success." And each generation that takes on this philosophy acquires more and more and more - particularly more depression, stress, body-fat, greed and entitlement, hopelessness, despair and anxiety disorders. If that is your goal, you are doing a fantastic job.

If however, what you want is a peace and security which is unaffected by the relentless changing of physical circumstances, a joy that is untouched by what the world calls loss, an inspired enthusiasm in doing the work that is set before you, a satisfaction and contentment in making use of your time and talents in ways that are most natural and pleasing to you . . . then, there is a whole other way to approach the living of your days. <u>You must learn to appreciate, enjoy and honor the days of small beginnings</u>. You must run with joyful patience the race that is set before you. You must learn to enjoy and make good use of what you have, no matter how "*small peanuts*" it may seem to be.

Tend your part of the garden with great loving-care and tenderness no matter how small it may seem to you - and even more than that, take pride in what has been given and achieved no matter how humble it may seem to you. Allow things to grow slowly in their own timing and way. We assure you that there is no competition in Spirit. <u>ONLY THE EGO EVER COMPETES AT ALL</u>! When you have even the slightest twinge of a feeling of competition and comparison that is always ego, no exceptions.

If you want to be "*of the spirit*" then release all others and release all comparisons. Bless the days of small beginnings and savor the time tending the garden as a "*walking meditation*" in which each and every act is done as a service to the Great Spirit within all things. This is the way to peace, satisfaction and joy in all your work, whether personal or professional. It is not about perfection, it is about progress. ENOY and SAVOR what you already have rather than endlessly straining to get more or to "improve" everything. On the day that you release the concept of improving from your mind, you will begin to find the peace, self-esteem and acceptance that you have been yearning for all this time.

Right here, right now, there are so many "little things" that if you would only take the time to give a some caring attention to would begin to feed your soul with joy and dissolve all those feelings of yearning, dissatisfaction and fear. Bless all the little things in your life today. The most amazing things in your world begin as quite small - embryos, flower seeds, and life-long friendships all start as very small things before growing into something beautiful and life-giving.

47. Work with the ENERGY

". . . but let me remind you that time and space are under my control." -A Course in Miracles

REMEMBER THAT EVERYTHING IS ABOUT ENERGY. Humans spend far too much time concerned with manipulating matter, people, conditions and situations instead of working with what really matters - the ENERGY that is present. Like the proverbial bull in a china shop, you often go charging in crashing up against opposing energies and vibrations because you have not first stopped to TUNE IN; to SENSE and work with the energies that are present. You become too interested in getting your way and making things happen the way YOU think would be best for all concerned.

Remember that the Universe is a friendly system. It wants to work WITH you as a cooperative agent in all situations and circumstances. But you must be willing and patient enough to slow down so that you can become attuned to the energies that are dominating. Then, rather than trying to conquer or push the energies, or manipulate them to your will, you can cooperate and begin to channel those energies through the Wisdom that is REVEALED to you by the Presence within you.

How to do this? RELAX, even if everyone else is whipped into a frenzy around you. If possible, close your eyes, even for an instant and say to the Presence within, *"Make good use of me here."* Then LISTEN to REALITY beyond appearances rather than the "story" ABOUT the appearances that the ego is endlessly chattering about to you - really LISTEN in the space. RESPOND to whatever spiritual intuition reveals to you and be willing to keep correcting as you go. Do not get attached to being right or to specific outcomes. BE FLUID, be flexible, be cooperative. Be persistent, but not pushy. Be consistent, but not pedantic.

There is a vast untapped Wisdom within you which awaits your attention and cooperation. Learn to work with the ENERGY rather than the personality and you will find that the doors and windows to your greater good are opening nearly everywhere you go.

48. A Problem Consciousness

"The opposite of love is fear, but what is all-encompassing can have no opposite. This course can therefore be summed up very simply in this way: Nothing real can be threatened. Nothing unreal exists. Here in lies the peace of God." -A Course in Miracles

ONE OF THE MAIN OBSTACLES to the peace and joy that you say you want is that you so easily lose track of where you are going. You say you are heading out for a day of miracles, peace, love and joy . . . but, then you can so easily lose track of that destination as you give your attention to the "annoying" person in line in front of you, the slowness of the other cars, the mess the baby made, the distressing call from the bank. And it is not that you should ignore these things - but it is the KIND of attention you PAY them that throws you off the highlighted route. In simple terms you give them your power and your joy. And this is because so often you have a "*problem-oriented*" consciousness rather than a "*miracle-minded*" Consciousness. Your very active mind has been trained to go into a situation and look for the danger rather than for the flowers.

Because the ego IS body-identification, it's main concern is the safety and survival of the "*body-as-self.*" This means it is always alert to ANYTHING it perceives as dangerous to it in any way - and it is wildly attracted to whatever it thinks will give it comfort, pleasure and gratification. This is an EXTREMELY stressful way to walk through the world. And this is why the main parts of the Course are about an unlearning and a mind training.

In the Christic Consciousness, there simply ARE no problems - "*what is all-encompassing can have no opposite.*" This means that it is not your task to go through each day and every situation looking for the problem that needs to be tackled, conquered and solved. It is not your task to endlessly seek out what you think you need for your safety, comfort and security every day. It is your task to remember God and cultivate THAT Divine Consciousness in which you walk into the room and focus your attention on the flowers, on the smiling face, on anything that there is to bless and praise. There is an inexorable drive towards Life, toward wholeness and renewal . . . even when it is only a blade of grass rising up through a crack in the dirty sidewalk. The flower, the blade of grass, has no "*intended results*" list, no "*story*" about how obstacles are stopping it, nor is it trying to whip itself into a "*peak performance*" mode; it simply goes around whatever seems to stand in the way of the Light it is nourished and fed by. It has a "*no problem*" Consciousness - and this is what We wish to bring out in you, because it is already there, inherent in your Divine Nature.

This means that the mess the baby made, the distressing call from the bank, the slow moving traffic - these are not problems; they are reminders to guide your own thoughts back to the God Consciousness as you remember our ceaselessly reminding you "*We've got this*." Turn within for Guidance on what to do, think, and say. SURRENDER it all to the Power that is in you, but not of you. EXPECT miracles today as you go about looking for the flowers in every room - and for every "sign" that God is on the Field and all is well.

49. Forgiveness Makes You Attractive

"Forgiveness offers everything I want." - A Course in Miracles

PERHAPS THAT YOU THINK the blessings of God are only the more "*spiritual*" states of being or are merely symbolic and metaphorical. This is simply not so. Though the egoic world is an illusion, We have discussed many times that it can be a nightmare illusion or the Holy Spirit within you can transform it into a "*happy dream.*" Sacrifice and suffering are the result of the "*ego's religions*" and have nothing to do the Infinite Friend that is the One true God. You were not born to struggle through life as a survivor; you were meant to thrive.

And you have also been reminded that the gifts of God are free, but that that does not mean they don't cost anything. The major cost of the life of THRIVING is forgiveness. In fact, forgiveness DOES offer everything you want. If you have any problem at all, it is most often a forgiveness problem. You may think it is a health problem, a money problem, a relationship problem or a work problem . . . but it is really a forgiveness problem. This is not only forgiveness of others and of yourself, but it is quite often forgiveness of the stressful concepts and untrue philosophies you cling to. Forgiveness is LETTING GO. Forgiveness means you are cancelling the debt - not because it is the spiritual thing to do but rather because it is the fastest path to what you truly want.

PLEASE stop making your relationship with Divine Presence such a solemn drag!!! God is the original author of FUN! Heaven is the state of JOY, remember?

In fact, you would do well to shake your forgiveness paradigm to the core by turning it entirely around. Instead of making it some HUGE difficult spiritual BURDEN that you feel you "*should*" do, make it the most fun of all. We strongly suggest you create your own unique personal AFFIRMATION/DECLARATION to use daily as part of "The Forgiveness Game" - perhaps something like,

> *I am quick to forgive because forgiveness makes me rich, sexy, successful and happy! The more I forgive, the hotter I get!*

Yes, We are telling you to FORGIVE FOR SELFISH REASONS!! Do not forget that the Teacher of God is generous out of self-interest. Forgiveness is the greatest beauty treatment and health regimen in the Cosmos! Of course the ego has many paths to riches, love, success, health and so on - and many of them work in reaching the desired end, but they are SO not fun and are ultimately unsatisfying. Remember, Life is not about the arriving at the destination; it's the fun of the journey that makes it all worthwhile.

If you spend just a few minutes considering this you will see the sense of it. Just do the math. Grievances and resentments tend to be a breeding ground for illnesses, poor aging, feelings of impoverishment, relationship and intimacy problems, work and career issues, and they make a person unattractive. It's really a no-brainer to realize that forgiveness is the neutralizing agent; the ultimate answer to these problems. Simply put, forgiveness makes you more attractive in the way you WANT to be attractive.

50. Stepping It Up

DEAREST MIRACLE WORKER, We fully intend to rock your personal world in the most wonderful ways if you will DO what it takes to let it happen. The question is, are you on board with the program? If not, We never force - We merely invite and create possibilities.

However, it will mean a real detachment from the world you SEE and a determination to keep your eyes on your own paper! LAW and Free Will still remain in effect so you will have to do your best to keep your vibration clear and to FOLLOW the natural Laws of Mind and Spirit. What you give is going to be of paramount importance - the vibrational seeds you sow are going to reap harvest after harvest so SOW

CAREFULLY. If you come at things only focused on what you NEED AND WANT, you will find a world that is needing and wanting FROM YOU - and usually that which you would prefer to keep for yourself. In particular here, We are thinking in terms of giving COMPLIMENTS, CREDIT, LOVING AKNOWLEDGMENT, GRATITUDE AND PRAISE.

This kind of giving is more important for this New Age than you can even begin to imagine as yet. As always, you will need help and assistance during this year and though it will come from God, it will come THROUGH human beings. And human beings whom you have not honored, thanked and praised consistently will not be too willing to be the vessel for you if you only call when you need help. The relationship "bank account" is one in which you need to focus more on DEPOSITS than on withdrawals!

YOU MUST get over being embarrassed by expressing intimate words of appreciation!! Are you praising your mate and children EVERY SINGLE DAY OF THE YEAR?! If not, start now. Do you THANK your employer for giving you work on a regular basis? Do you accept encouragement and inspiration without regularly showing gratitude? Are you in the habit of taking what is offered as some kind of personal metaphysical "manifestation" and then not thanking the vessel through which it came? Do you thank the trees and flowers you see along your pathways? Do you thank the sky and the grass? We know you think this is ridiculous, but We cannot tell you how very serious we are about this and how profoundly GRATITUDE can rock your world in this new phase you are entering. What you are not thanking and praising will begin to disappear from your personal experience in this time of Higher Consciousness. Remember, the object of attention RECEIVES ENERGY and increases. Consciousness animates matter.

You can look around and see what is being fed with attention - expect more reality shows of people fighting and going after meaningless things, more famous people who have no talent and nothing of any value to offer, more violent dark movies, more humor based on depression and negativity, financial "cliffs," more competition for finite resources, more belief in the victim consciousness that dominates the planet.

But YOU can experience an entirely different world if you are willing to SOW SEEDS every single day in your own garden. This will require HUMILITY at the time when arrogance is higher on the planet than We have ever known it to be. You will need to GIVE the very things you want most if you are to have a Divine Harvest. You will need to give them to others and TO YOURSELF! This is not easy for the ego. People will seem to steal your ideas, take advantage of you, take the credit, pass you by . . . this is TEMPORARY and will only continue if you FOCUS ON IT AND TELL THE STORY OF IT. AND it means that you will need to start giving credit where credit is due if you expect a harvest of like energy in your own life.

If you can let Us Help you in this, this will be a year of the gentle steady blossoming of your Garden in the most abundant and glorious ways imaginable. But again, you must keep your eyes ON YOUR SIDE OF THE FENCE, IN YOUR YARD, ON YOUR OWN GARDEN. The time of Grace is upon you now if you can keep on taking the steps in Consciousness necessary. If you have not already, UP your gratitude game tremendously! Start praising those who are part of your daily world - particularly those you tend to take most for granted or whom you think owe YOU some gratitude. Do NOT forget to include yourself in this - you owe yourself a tremendous debt of gratitude and praise! If you IGNORE caring for yourself, you will burn out and not be in any position to receive all the good! Before anything blossoms in your garden you will have given much time and energy to watering, weeding, fertilizing and patiently waiting, not in faith but in KNOWLEDGE of Principle.

We know, ego HATES this - that's why it's GRADUATE LEVEL spiritual practice. And that is also why the fruits of this kind of practice are so much juicier and nutritious than any other kind of practice. It's time to step-up your game again. This is the perfect time to reflect on those human vessels through whom you have received blessings this year - do not let the sun go down today before you have praised, honored and acknowledged these beings in your own heart and mind.

51. *Calm Down & Cheer Up*

"Simplicity is very difficult for twisted minds." - A Course in Miracles

TRY NOT TO TRY SO HARD, dear ones. We appreciate and maximize your efforts to the degree that you allow Us to - and the way you allow Us to is by getting out of the way, following the Intuition We give you, and keeping your eyes on your own paper. Yes, We want you to pay attention, but We do not want you overthinking everything quite so much. When We encourage you to relax, this is not about cultivating unconsciousness or carelessness. It is actually a focused awareness - but on your own business. Struggling so hard to get it right, to figure things out, to be the perfect student or practitioner - this is valiant and yet hopeless. There is an easier way. Let's call it, *"Do your best and forget the rest"* as We've heard one of your physical trainers say it. It's not necessary to hit a home run every single time. There can even be joy in striking out if you have the proper attitude about the game.

You make it very complicated when it is really quite simple, simple, simple. Don't try to be God. Let God be God. Enjoy the ride more. Savor the moments, the days, the people. Help Us Help you. Come inside to the Temple more frequently throughout the day for very short periods of time. Let Us soothe and uplift you with Our words and Our Energy. If you want to make a change, ask Us about it - and when you receive the Answer, act on it with a calm cheerful energy as best you can. Keep a positive attitude and refuse to whine, worry or complain. Pet the cat. Adopt a rescue dog. Walk in nature more. Sing HAPPY songs very loud when you are alone in the car. Clear out a little bit of clutter each day. Strike up conversations with strangers. Offer to help a friend out. Ask for some help. Let the sun shine on your face for a few minutes each day.

The journey is ruined when you are anxiously chanting *"are we there yet, are we there yet, are we there yet?"*

52. Perceiving Joy

"Every thought you have makes up some segment of the world you see. It is with your thoughts, then, that we must work, if your perception of the world is to be changed." -A Course in Miracles

THE FIRST AND MOST SIGNIFICANT HEALING will always be the healing of your own mind; healing of your perceptions and your mental habit patterns. This precedes every true and lasting change of the physical. Seek first then, to have your mind be healed and lifted to a higher level of Consciousness even as you go about making positive changes in your behavior or in the external. Rather than be obsessed with the question of *"what should I DO???"* - begin with the question, *"what should I think? To Whom shall I turn?"* And then turn swiftly within and seek Guidance.

Turning within is not the solemn "religious" experience some of you make it out to be. True turning within is an experience of great joy, peace, relief, inspiration and soothing. <u>Remember that the Kingdom of Heaven IS Joy</u> - so turning to the Kingdom Within IS turning to the state of Joy. More and more We have been assisting you in thinking more JOYFULLY. We want you to begin to acknowledge the progress that you have made.

Rather than focusing on how much farther you have to go, take some time today to honor how far you have traveled on this journey of EXPANDED Consciousness. The fact that every thought you have is not an uplifted God-like thought of faith and positivity is not significant to Us. What IS significant is how many MORE God-like faith-filled positive thoughts you have than you once did. What impresses Us is how you are willing to turn ego thoughts around much more quickly now and how much MORE joy you are allowing into your perceptions.

You have stopped trudging around the bottom of the mountain, endlessly repeating the old patterns of thinking and perceiving. You are now steadily taking those penguin steps with us UP the mountain - AND you are allowing yourself to enjoy the journey so much more! Yes, We have planned much more expansion for you, much more healing, and many more positive changes in the ways that you think and behave - but, We are all about gentle steady change. This begins with AWARENESS and a kindly observation of yourself. Remember that We are "*training the puppy*" rather than whipping the horse. Breathe that in dear Urban Mystic. Today is a significant day in your training, not only for yourself, but for all those who will be touched by your Consciousness. Think deliberately today, but do so very gently and with non-attachment. We will make JOYFUL use of you today to the extent that you simply get out of the way and LET Us open the right doors and close the wrong ones.

All is well - simply show up, prepared, on time, doing

what you said you would do, with a GOOD attitude. We'll handle the rest.

53. No Scarcity, No Lack

"It is only because you think you can run some small part, or deal with certain aspects of your life alone, that the guidance of the Holy Spirit is limited." -A Course in Miracles

YOU STILL DON'T FULLY RECOGNIZE how much of your thinking and living is rooted in the "*scarcity principle*" which the ego teaches - and it is not really a principle at all but rather another illusion of fear. What this creates within you is a defensiveness and a "*covering your ass*" in such a way that you are often busy, busy, busy, without being particularly fruitful as you run around physically and mentally trying to accomplish, accomplish, accomplish - as if you there is an end to that "to do" list of yours.

Remember, miracles are a means of saving time so that time can be used to more mutual benefit to you, those in your life and to The Plan. For all the "time-saving" devices that humans have created, many of you tend to feel more rushed and overwhelmed than ever before. This is always how the ego thought system works - it actually increases or creates the very thing it is meant to "get rid of." This need not be.

Periodically throughout your day, STOP and remind yourself to drop your defenses and your Lone Ranger mentality. ASK for Us to guide you in whatever is the next portion of your day - let your shoulders drop, open up and relax your hands - you may even want to gently put your palms up, softly hold them out as you mentally say to yourself, *"I am asking for Guidance and I am open to receive it now."* Remember, there is no shortage of anything. We have ALL the resources you need for whatever you truly need, and for what would be most helpful. There is no need for you to struggle to do everything or even *anything* all by yourself. When you join with Spirit, you begin to understand the Principle of *"effortless accomplishment"* in which you can be fruitful and busy when you WANT to be - in ways that feel invigorating and good to you rather than exhausting and depleting.

It is amazing how resistant to love, peace and joy you sometimes still are - and how much you prefer to cling to struggle and suffering as if there were some morality prize for those who suffer the most. Let it go. It has no value except to see the contrast and realize again that you do not really want to suffer or struggle. Keep it simple miracle worker. LET it be simple because it really is.

54. Grace for Today

"Spirit is in a state of grace forever. Your reality is only spirit. Therefore you are in a state of grace forever." -A Course in Miracles

DEAR MIRACLE WORKER - as always, our deepest Intention is to Help you to enjoy not only your everyday life, but also the process of learning your lessons in this curriculum. Help is ever-present and as plentiful as the air you breathe in and out all day long.

When you become fearful, you have a tendency to become very shallow breathers, even though more breath would be the very thing to help calm you and release the negative vibrations. In this very same way, fear often "seizes" you up in a way that keeps you from the awareness of Our Presence surrounding you. Relaxing into Our Essence is exactly what can alleviate the fear and constriction.

The kind of clinging that fear produces IS the problem. And quite often what you are clinging to the most is what is blocking you from receiving all the Grace and gifts which would flow into your hands if they were empty. We cannot fill hands that are white-knuckled fists grasping to keep hold of "the *little that they have*." Have you not seen the seemingly homeless people walking your streets with grocery store carts full of their "treasures" of scraps of paper, plastic bags, rotting fabrics and containers which hold nothing? Many of you have mental grocery carts full of the very same kinds of meaningless empty useless ideas and concepts which you use all your strength to push through your life day after day after day.

Let it all go today dear friend. Surrender all to the Grace of the day and know that there will be more Grace tomorrow and the next day and the next and for every tomorrow after that. We've got you covered, IF you will relax and ALLOW it to be. Think less about tomorrow's daily bread as you are enjoying today's. "Knock" and "ask" are very good advice indeed, but give up hammering against the doors or mistaking whining and bargaining with asking.

Relax - We've got this. Offer yourself to Him to be used today to be joyfully Helpful and then go about your business and sure enough, We will send you to the right people and places where you can be most helpful. And while you are busy being distracted from your own worries, We'll finally have a chance to work on your life for you without your interference and micro-managing.

55. *The World*

*"This is an insane world, and do not underestimate the extent of it's insanity. There is no area of your perception that it has not touched, and your dream IS sacred to you. That is why God placed the Holy Spirit in you, where you placed the dream." -*A Course in Miracles

AREN'T YOU GLAD to know that the world you see is insane? You should be. If you take the world of your TV news seriously and try to understand the insanity of it, YOU will drive yourself crazy. That world cannot be understood, figured out or fixed. It is not the real world and those who expend so much of their energy trying to repair the illusion only end up enraged and deeply depressed. Many misguided "spiritual teachers" have walked the planet in great sadness, trying to teach salvation. If that is not insane, what is?

Only joyful love heals, and it is the purpose of His Course to heal your mind of the belief that the world of illusions can bring you either happiness or sorrow. Remember, enlightenment is a recognition of what has always been present; it is not an actual change. Enlightenment recognizes Truth and Reality even in the midst of an insane world of illusions. And enlightenment without JOY, is not enlightenment at all. Guilt and fear over the world you see is the evidence that the ego has managed to make you forget about the Love that heals all illusions.

It is true that when you help another, you are growing closer to your own Divine nature, but it must be non-attached giving that does not attempt to "fix" but rather only to share - and how can you share something you do not have? The Holy Spirit IS here with you now and will guide you as much as you will allow so that you can save time and avoid suffering. A suffering worried savior is no help whatsoever. <u>YOU must be happy in order to extend happiness</u>. YOU must be sane in order to extend sanity. YOU must BE aware of Love in order to extend Love.

YOUR Joy, peace and happiness today is what you have to offer in order to reveal the real world that exists just beyond the mists. There is much to be happy about, much to celebrate, much to honor, much to praise. Start now by invoking that which brings the most joyful vibrations to your own Consciousness. This will function as a Lighthouse for those who are ready to find and accept the Love that heals. That's all - simply shine your own Light and more and more you will find that the insane world of illusions has no power over you. Today is YOUR day of freedom, sanity, peace and Joy!

56. You Already Have It

"Peace I leave with you, my peace I give unto you: not as the world giveth, give I unto you. Let not your heart be troubled, neither let it be afraid." - John 14:27

OFTEN YOU WASTE YOUR ENERGY and time praying for that which is already yours. You are focused on getting rather than receiving. Much of what you want to get you already have, but you have not done what is necessary to ACCEPT it. The box remains wrapped-up over in the corner, rather than being opened and used as it was intended.

PEACE IS ALREADY YOURS. You will never have one bit more peace than you have right now in this very moment. ALL the peace in the entire Cosmos has already been given to you, but you cannot know this when you are not activating it within you. If through your thoughts and attention you are activating the vibrational frequencies of fear, worry, dread, confusion, scarcity, grief, anger, attack, defensiveness and all the other lower vibrations of the ego-dominated worldview - well, you've left your gift of PEACE sitting off in the corner gathering dust. Remember, getting and receiving are two different things entirely. There is much that you have "gotten" and not yet received.

Today, right now, and ALWAYS for that matter, you have the opportunity to activate the Peace that has been given you. But you must STOP your frantic searching and flailing and allow your mind to grow quiet and still. You must learn to become a gracious receiver - one who not only "gets" but who then receives and uses what has been given. If you choose, today can be a day in which you walk the world AS a beacon of Divine Light unto the world. As you activate, extend and share the Peace that has been given you, it becomes stronger and more alive within you. What glorifies the Creator is the USE of the gifts given. Additionally, to whom much has been given and used, much MORE is given. DO NOT HOARD MANNA! Happily and gratefully USE UP what you have and more will continue to flow in! The branch that does not bear fruit is CUT OFF and cast into the garbage. Please be a branch that is bearing fruit through the ACCEPTANCE, ACTIVATION and USE of all the gifts of God.

Here is a way to begin - take a deep breath, let your thoughts slow down, relax the mind and body - then turn within and say,

"Father Mother God, I accept and receive Your gifts now and it is my

> *intention to use them with joy and gratitude for myself and for those who come into my circle of Consciousness today. Help me to make joyful use of Your gifts to me today."*

Then, simply bless all those who cross your path or your mind today whether you believe they deserve it or not. Imagine that you are scattering and sowing seeds of Light all across your path today and that these seeds transform all that they touch. As you do so you are literally extending Peace, and what you extend, you strengthen within yourself. ACCEPT what has already been given dear Miracle Worker. We have much more to give once you begin to make better use of what you already have. THIS is a very auspicious day for you if you will allow it to be so. We are SO happy for you and so ready to Help you. The gift has already been given - what will you make of it today?

57. Mind Yoga

"If thou canst believe, all things are possible to him that believeth." - Mark 9:23

THOUGHTS RISE AND FALL in your awareness in a constant flow all through the day and night. A dizzying amount of those thoughts may be extremely negative, stressful or fearful. That in itself does not matter. It is only the thoughts that you BELIEVE that have a real and lasting effect on you and your life.

You may talk a good metaphysical game or go around spouting 12 step mottos all day long, but there is nothing quite so cheap as talk. What REALLY matters, what really creates the harvest in your life, is what you are BELIEVING deep in the quiet of your own soul and in your own mind.

And ultimately, it must be PERSONAL. What do YOU believe is possible for <u>YOU</u>? If you believe that miracles are possible for others, that your children can have a wonderful future, that certain people have the talent, background and courage to live a successful life, but you have somehow excluded yourself from that reality, then IT IS DONE UNTO YOU AS YOU BELIEVE and you yourself have sealed the doors by which you might have stepped into God's greater Will for you.

Do you believe it is too late for you? Have you stopped dreaming? Have you died before your time? The word repent means to turn around. There may be areas of your life where you need to repent - to turn around. It starts with thought. It is true that the journey of 1,000 miles begins with a single step. Anyone can take a single step, and then another, and then another. Even if you have legs that do not move, that no longer work, you can take a single step in Consciousness, in attitude, in willingness.

What do you BELIEVE is possible for you? Find out. Investigate. Look inside and ask the questions. And know that whatever you believe is possible is merely your starting point. With God, all things are possible and you can begin to expand beyond those self-imposed limitations right now.

You can start this week by practicing this little exercise of saying to yourself, *"I am starting to believe _____."* Just keep filling in the blank, over and over and over again. It's yoga for the mind. And if even that is too big a step for you, start with *"I WANT to believe that* _____.*"* This can be the bridge that then carries you to STARTING to believe which then leads to the actual believing. You CAN start from wherever you are, right here, right now.

58. The Regeneration Program

"I am not a body. I am free." - A Course in Miracles

WE WANT TO REMIND YOU that your body is merely a projection of your state of mind. It is changing all the time as a reflection of some aspect of your Consciousness. And so it is time for NEW THOUGHTS to arise to supplant your old limiting ideas and beliefs about the body.

It is easiest to begin this by allowing Us to download the "Regeneration Program" into your Consciousness as soon as possible. It's a simple download and We can do it while your body slumbers at night. All you need to do is get in bed, close your eyes, take some easy compassionate breaths and say, *"I am now traveling to Source Headquarters. You may begin the download of the Regeneration Program as soon as I fall asleep."* We will handle all the rest of it. We do the prep work of starting to erase old erroneous thoughts about aging, disease, family genetics, and so on and then We will easily download all the new systems.

Keep in mind, the Consciousness of your planet is shifting and many of you will live over 100 Earth years in these bodies, but only if you have the BELIEF system that allows it to be so. Your body is already changing all the time and the body you are living in now is NOT old at all - none of it was here a decade ago. It is all new material. The body is in a constant state of metamorphosis as old cells die and are released and new ones come into being. Your body is ALWAYS young and youthful - ALWAYS. But your Consciousness programs it to create new cells that look and act old - BECAUSE OF YOUR BELIEF THAT AGING IS INEVITABLE.

The Regeneration Program is a "fix" for that; it assists you in creating new cells that are vital, energetic, strong, youthful and able. This is a fix to your DNA longevity programming and it can also erase and dump old genetic programming geared toward disease and decline. YOUR part after the download is to begin to REMEMBER and DAILY AFFIRM that you and your body are friends, not enemies, and that it knows how to repair, rejuvenate, regenerate and that it is coded to be a useful vessel for as long as your Spirit chooses to use it. <u>NEVER speak negatively about your body because your body takes it as an ORDER to DO whatever you are saying about it. SPEAK ONLY LOVE about your body and BELIEVE only the very best about it</u>. It will reward you with good health, energy, vitality and congenial companionship.

59. Fear Fast, Kindness Feast

"I have saved all your kindnesses and every loving thought you ever had. I have purified them of the errors that hid their light, and kept them for you in their own perfect radiance." - A Course in Miracles

IT'S TIME FOR YOU TO REST in the comfort of the Holy Spirit for a season. The ego has an endless drive toward complication and mental gymnastics. Truth is far simpler than all of that. Return to the Source, to the root where you can gather up the nourishment and spiritual food that you need in order to bear good fruit in due season.

For now, all you need do is focus on kindness as the major part of your spiritual practice. Try now to think of love as an ACTIVE Force, rather than a feeling. Think less about the emotion and merely focus on BEING KIND. Begin at home, with yourself, each morning. Feed, dress and bathe yourself with ultimate kindness and attention. Then, let it ripple out from there.

As much as we cajole and tease you in these lessons, We also want to remind you that We have observed that humans are inherently kind, generous and truly giving. It is the indistinguishable spark of the Spirit within that is actually dominant even on your dense Earth plane. Yes dominant, or you would not have the billions of humans living on the Earth today. So, We are encouraging you to KNOW this and connect with this Truth which is rarely shown on your news channels. Peace IS dominant, but fear has a much more aggressive marketing campaign. Lies need defending and a PR machine to keep the ball in play. Eternal Truth needs no defense, and the only campaign Truth has is *"listen, learn and DO."*

So during this season of learning, let your DOing be primarily a simple mantra of "BE KIND." Keep it nice and simple this semester of your life by fasting from fearful strategies while you return to the simplicity of Source Energy by knowing that if you forget every other spiritual lesson completely, you CAN easily remember to put kindness first.

60. Keep Your Appointment

"The problem is not one of concentration; it is the belief that no one,

including yourself, is worth consistent effort." - A Course in Miracles

WHERE YOU FALL DOWN is where you will have to get up. You cannot fall down at the bottom of the mountain, but stand up at the peak. The journey happens one patient methodical, often boring, step at a time. This is very difficult for a generation geared toward instant gratification and the desire for applause at every step forward. When you were a toddler you received praise and applause for every step forward - even when you fell down on your butt.

But those days are long over now. You are not spiritual babies anymore. <u>This means you must be your own cheering section instead of your own critic</u>. We are here to cheer you on, but often you want another HUMAN to notice and give you a pat on the back - which is looking to the outside for validation. It's lovely when it happens, but to count on it is just another ego addiction. <u>Progress is made during the mundane boring times of life when no one is watching</u>; showing up at the meditation mat, at the gym, cleaning out the garage, making the better food choices, doing your mirror work, saying something kind and real instead of snarky, doing your affirmations in the car instead of having imaginary arguments or worried fantasies. All of these are appointments you make with yourself and far too often humans tend to cancel appointments with the self at the drop of a hat in order to keep a far less important appointment with someone else, or with the TV, or with a negative whining conversation.

We are not talking about "putting yourself first" because that is an entirely ego concept of "either or." This is precisely the kind of finite limited thinking the ego specializes in. Remember, Our NEW thoughts have to do with the elasticity of time and space - limitless possibilities. You don't have to know HOW right now. <u>First, make the commitment</u>

and THEN the possibilities begin to emerge. It's NOT the other way around.

REMOVE guilt and "shoulds" from this process entirely. They are of NO value whatsoever and are also ego tools which will only delay progress. Know that you will make mistakes and fall down - so what? You simply stand up right where you fell down and then take the next step. No shame. No blame.

Consider the amount of time that an Olympic athlete spends in boring daily workouts compared to the time spent standing on a pedestal with a medal on her chest. You must become your own daily cheering section and give yourself a medal every time you show up for your appointments with yourself. The best way to do this is to begin to savor and enjoy even the "boring" moments of life. Tell yourself a better story and CHOOSE to enjoy the journey instead of telling yourself that it's hard, that you don't like it, that it's taking too long, that no one appreciates your efforts, that you're going to fail anyhow, that it's selfish to be doing this . . . and on into infinity. Tell yourself,

> *"I enjoy the process of positive change. I can do this. There is no hurry about any of this. I am learning as I go. I am worth showing up for. Small positive changes are still important changes. I am happily going in the right direction now."*

You ARE worth the effort. We can tell you that forever and a day, but YOU are the one who needs to begin to say it to yourself. And if you are not yet in that place, go ahead and act as if you believe it by showing up and playing the part of a person who does. Yes, PRETEND. And if you play pretend long enough, it will start to feel true, and with time and practice it WILL be true.

61. *The Treasure House*

"My treasure house is full, and angels watch its open doors that not one gift is lost, and only more are added. Let me come to where my treasures are, and enter in where I am truly welcome and at home, among the gifts that God has given me." - A Course in Miracles

COME! COME TO THE TREASURE HOUSE and RECEIVE YOUR gifts today. We bow down to welcome you with love and happy service to the One Who has filled this space and Who gives all Life so abundantly. There is nothing you need do to earn these precious treasures - or they would not be gifts. They await your recognition that they have already been given. Too often you are asking, asking, asking for what has already been given.

Yet here your gifts are already carefully placed, in the Treasure House Within. Yes, all the peace, the Power, the joy, the love, wholeness, wisdom, direction and so much more await your recognition and the courage and boldness to actually activate and USE what has been given. Healing the sick, raising the dead, pulling coins from the mouths of fishes, manna falling from the sky - greater things than these are possible to anyone who is willing to mentally step away from the endless droning and humming of the physical world in order to enter the Realm that is hidden just behind the Mists.

At this time in your history, the veil between realities is quite thin, which means there has never been a more auspicious time to demonstrate to yourself that you are under no laws but God's. Think of something while you are within the Treasure House and it appears, whether you call it bad or good. Therefore, fill your mind with visions of the world you want to create for yourself and you have immediately begun activating the building blocks of your own reality. Your Consciousness animates matter and a withdrawal of Consciousness causes the collapse of matter into other forms.

Whatever is good, true and lovely - think on these things today - activate them and know that they are a part of the gifts in your own Treasure House waiting for you to open, use and enjoy. Practice being a gracious receiver today for it honors the Giver of the gifts.

62. A Better Choice

"Trials are but lessons that you failed to learn presented once again, so where you made a faulty choice before you can now make a better one, and thus escape all pain that what you chose before has brought to you. In every difficulty, all distress, and each perplexity Christ calls to you and gently says, 'My brother, choose again.'" - A Course in Miracles

MAKE IT EASY ON YOURSELF Miracle Worker - slow down and pay more kind attention to what is right in front of you in your now. This does not mean that you cannot make plans for later today, tomorrow, or next week if that is the wisdom that comes forth. But what We are reminding you of in this moment is how many of your mistakes come from not PAYING ATTENTION to this moment. Paying more gentle attention in your now allows you to see a lesson arising in the moment it arises so that the Holy Instant expands leaving a wonderful gap between stimulus and response. In THAT gap, you can make a better and more Conscious choice from love instead of fear.

Remember that your unique curriculum is not at random. YOU very carefully chose it yourself at another level and now it is time to learn it - and you CAN learn it joyously if you are WILLING to let go of your ego attachments. You don't "get rid of" the attachments, but simply observe them and CHOOSE not to invest there – then, they often simply dissolve over time. This happens one thought at a time, one moment at a time, one choice at a time. Also remember, you are an EXCELLENT student and have made tremendous progress this time around. Keep this in your heart and KNOW the Truth of it. Do NOT let the ego steal your joy over some story that you are a terrible student who cannot learn the lesson before you.

Do not become frustrated when lessons are repeated over and over again at times. At this point in your learning it is rarely because you made a terrible choice the last time but rather only that there is still room for improvement. Once a toddler reaches the point where she is no longer falling down while walking, she continues to improve for many years and can become not merely a functional walker but quite graceful and elegant if done with thoughtfulness and CONSCIOUSNESS. At first, it may be "self-consciousness" and self-doubt, but with enough positive reinforcement and practice, it becomes effortless and natural.

Take some time with us today and in the coming days to go inside and reflect with Spirit, not with ego. Look to see where you have made progress in your "better choices" and look to see where you would like to learn to make better choices. Make love, peace and joy your goals in this. These are the kinds of choices that are "better" - the ones that lead to more love, peace and joy in your daily walk. Love for self and for others - remember it is "*love your neighbor AS yourself.*"

63. *Help is Here*

"It will never happen that you will have to make decisions for yourself. You are not bereft of help, and Help that knows the answer." - A Course in Miracles

IF WE HAD AN EGO, it would be insulting to Us to see how often you worry while We are right here beside you ready to Help. Humans have a strange tendency to shut out Source and then writhe around feeling separate and afraid. When you allow yourself to worry, this is exactly what you are doing, denying access to the Answer, taking on life all alone and then feeling overwhelmed and terrified. This need not be.

You simply MUST relax in order to experience miracles. They cannot come through in an atmosphere of struggle, manipulation and fear. LET GO miracle worker! Do not let go into chaos and uncertainty - LET GO INTO the Infinite Stream of God's perfect Grace.

Remember that the development of trust is one of the first and most major lessons in the path of any miracle worker. If you are worrying, you are once again trying to lean on your own human strength and cleverness rather than trusting in Ours. Worry slows down and interferes with the natural process of the Divine unfolding of your good. Let your mind rest in God today. Relax and breathe, relax and breathe, relax and breathe. Stop waiting for the Cosmic Cavalry to ride in and save you. You are ALREADY saved right now if you can only see with the Spiritual Eye instead of the physical one - even if only for brief respites during the day today. Give up the illusion of control and SURRENDER as you let go of frantically mentally searching for some SIGN that help is on the way. It is here already, waiting for you to acknowledge and activate it by simply TRUSTING that even now, all things are held perfectly in the hands of God.

64. *Right Here, Right Now*

"Your little effort and small determination call on the power of the universe to help you, and God Himself will raise you from darkness into Light." - A Course in Miracles

RIGHT HERE, RIGHT NOW, as it pertains to your life, all things are held perfectly in the Hands of God. That is, unless you have taken matters into your own hands again.

We will never fight you. This is what free will is about - you are the chooser. You decide. There is no assertion from an outer authority in the sky. YOU determine which road of Consciousness to take each day. YOU are the authority - you are the programmer.

However, you are also perfectly free to surrender your authority to a Higher Authority each day - One Who loves you beyond all measure and reason. This is the One Who understands just what "greater good" actually means. One Who KNOWS you intimately and understands you better than you understand yourself; One Who is well aware of all of your weaknesses as well as your strengths - the obvious ones and those you've hidden even from yourself.

This kind of surrender is a giving up, a letting go, a happy and joyous resignation from running the show and from the need to try to manipulate and control anyone or anything. It is not a sad resignation at all. It is not a surrender to chaos and disorder. Quite the contrary. YOUR mortal way is the way of chaos and disorder. The mortal way is the daily building a castle in the sand which is washed away each night by the rising tides. Then, each morning you begin again another hopeless attempt to create a "permanent" refuge in the ephemeral.

We are inviting you to give up the fight today and to resist the temptation to "*hit the ground running.*" There IS another way, a better way, a happier way - a way of peace and joy and seemingly effortless accomplishment of good. JOIN with Us today and with the Great Crusade to activate the joy and peace that is the Divine Inheritance of every child of God.

Release what you think "should" be happening today and instead, tune into the Energy that IS present today. Go within periodically throughout the day for even a few seconds, tune into the vibrations, and ASK for Guidance and Help for every little thing (and big thing) that you do or think about today. We WANT to Help you, WANT to make the way straight and WANT to save you time and energy. But We will NOT fight nor argue with you. We do not try to FORCE you to trust Us. Free will means, you are the chooser of what world you will live in today. Choose, and then if you need to, choose as often as need be to continue to live in the world that YOU find most beneficial. We're on permanent standby.

65. *Turn It Around*

"There is nothing to fear . . . The presence of fear is a sure sign that you are trusting in your own strength. The awareness that there is nothing to fear shows that somewhere in your mind, though not necessarily a place you recognize as yet, you have remembered God, and let His strength take the place of your weakness." - A Course in Miracles

THE WORD "REPENT" means to "turn around." It is turning away from darkness, toward the Light. It is turning away from fear, and toward peace. This is what we are gently guiding you toward today Miracle Worker.

Whatever stressful story you may have going about your past, present or future, we invite you to begin now to gently turn it around. A NEW Thought neutralizes and dissolves an opposing thought. Thoughts of love neutralize and dissolve thoughts of fear. Thoughts of release neutralize and dissolve thoughts of attack and defensiveness. Thoughts of abundance and prosperity dissolve thoughts of lack and limitation. <u>With Our Help, you can turn around any stressful thought</u> - and you may begin by remembering that in God, all things are possible for you. You are not bound by the puny "laws" of this illusory world for in your TRUE world, miracles are commonplace and Grace is your natural state. What is broadcast on the evening news has nothing to do with YOUR world for you live in the Kingdom of Joy Within.

WATCH YOUR WORDS TODAY MIRACLE WORKER. The life and world you describe, whether past, present or future, is formed BY YOUR OWN WORDS. And you will be the heir of the exact words that you speak. <u>You SPEAK your world into existence</u> and your thinking fills it with emotion. Be diligent in creating your world with love, peace, joy and abundant good.

The decline into old age is NOT a the result of the body falling apart - it is a result of becoming fascinated by every symptom and serial adventure of the body. Talking about every ache and pain, every symptom, every procedure, each medicine taken, the loss of this or that activity, and about how things are not good enough now or how the "world" used to be better when you were younger . . . THIS is what creates an old person. <u>Speak of LIFE, and in that moment, you are young</u>. Speak of what you CAN do, rather than what you can no longer do. <u>Speak of what feels GOOD, instead of what feels bad. Speak of progress, rather than of decline.</u> REFUSE to stop learning and growing. <u>There has never been a better time to be alive on Planet Earth than right now</u>. Take advantage of this time and of all that is there for you to use.

You can speak of the wrong of your past, or you can choose to focus on the positive aspects of everyone and everything from your past. You can choose to believe that you were denied what you wanted, or you can choose to believe that you were simply spared what was not for your highest good. You can focus on where your parents got it wrong, or where they got it right. You can focus on what you've lost, or what you've gained. You can think of yourself as limited, or you can think of yourself as an ever-evolving creator and artist of LIFE! You can go drab, or you can go colorful! You can say, *"It's too hard!"* or you can say, *"I am willing."* YOU are the chooser, YOU are the programmer. You can turn it all around. You can repent in any instant that you turn away from fear and toward the Peace of God.

66. Help Us Help YOU!

"This course is a beginning, not an end. Your Friend goes with you. You are not alone. No one who calls on Him can call in vain. Whatever troubles you, be certain that He has the answer, and will gladly give it to you, if you simply turn to Him and ask it of Him." - A Course in Miracles

WORRY AND FEAR ARE SURE SIGNS that you are still trying to go it alone somehow. It is usually a sign that you are trying to control the externals, while not controlling your thinking much at all. Miracles are the result of the exact opposite equation. It is YOUR MIND which you must learn to control, while leaving all the rest to Us to handle for you. You still leave your mind unguarded far too much of the time.

Remember, this is a Course in MIND TRAINING, not a course in controlling the universe and getting what you think you want. You take YOU with you wherever you go, and if you have not learned to rule your mind when you have little of what you want, it will only get worse when you have much of what you want. If you are anxious and worried when living in a one room apartment, you'll be a worried anxious person in a mansion. YOU will not change just because the scenery is different. YOU will change when you decide to take responsibility for the nature of your thinking and begin guiding yourself to the thoughts that give more life, more peace, more possibilities and breathing space.

And this is about progress, not perfection. Backsliding happens. The point is simply to make the correction and proceed in the RIGHT direction. There is no need for guilt or blame. In particular, DO NOT DEFEND or explain why you fell down in the dirt. Just get up, have a little laugh at the ego, and continue on. There is no need for punishment or to do penance. Make any apologies or corrections necessary and then move on and LET IT GO. Remember that the Universe is ready to start again AT ANY MOMENT. And We can easily make up whatever time may have been "lost" - remember that time and space are under His control IF YOU WILL SIMPLY TURN IT OVER to the Christ Consciousness.

There is a wonderful day all planned out for you - are you willing to receive it without judgment? YOUR part is simply to DECIDE how you want to FEEL - to set a POSITIVE goal in terms of your thinking; for your thinking will determine your feelings. The ego has no positive goal at all - it simply wants to steal your joy in the moment by tempting you to think apart from Source. DO NOT ALLOW THIS TO HAPPEN. CHOOSE what you will focus on and think about today. We strongly suggest that at the top of each hour you focus on GRATITUDE, GRATITUDE, GRATITUDE for any and everything that you can think of - that you focus on the POSITIVE ASPECTS of your now. Give all your problems to Us to solve and if We need for you to get involved, you'll be Guided BECAUSE of your surrender to the Light. All is truly well.

67. Judging the Path

" . . . for you cannot distinguish between advance and retreat. Some of your greatest advances you have judged as failures, and some of your deepest retreats you have evaluated as success." - A Course in Miracles

OF COURSE YOU HAVE MESSED UP along the way. Of course others in your life have messed up along the way.

Welcome to the planet! This realm specializes in errors, mistakes, mess ups and misperceptions. That is not an excuse, but it is the way of things here. It is no reason to feel hopelessness and despair - nor is it a reason to not put forth your best efforts. It is part of the learning process. The reason We are bringing this up is so that you can release the tendency you sometimes have to judge your path and the paths of those around you.

Remember, to the Holy Spirit, even deep errors can be used as a part of the journey home to God - IF they are SURRENDERED and released. The errors that you keep, chew on, ruminate on for years - whether yours or another's - these keep you stuck in the wheel of cause and effect, grinding out misery in the present for something which is often in the distant past, or even earlier this week.

The Miracle happens in your NOW, in the instant that you are ready to let it go. No Miracle Worker has perfect behavior or thinking. If she did, she would not be useful on this plane of existence for true teaching and learning can only happen between those who are somewhat equal. A perfect being is too far vibrationally in Consciousness for any mortal to relate to and learn from. This is not justification to surrender to your ego impulses, but is the reason to surrender all your mistakes to the Comforter to be gently undone. Remember, Miracles are retroactive and restorative. Your past didn't even happen the way you think it did. Memory is not a recorder and it does not replay crisp clear images as you sometimes think it does.

Trust Us more than your faulty memories of a past which was written on the sand. We know you NOW and we are working with you TODAY to the extent that you let Us in. There is in fact, far more to learn from where you got it right than from where you got it wrong - far more to learn from where others got it right, than from where they fell down in the dirt. But ALL of it can be transformed into Light in the Divine Hands if you are willing to, in any moment, LET IT ALL GO AND MOVE ON.

Today is your day. There is much We have to do through you and for you. But you must be PRESENT to win!

68. Your Partner

"It is vain to worship idols in the hope of peace. God dwells within, and your completion lies in Him. No idol takes His place. Look not to idols. Do not seek outside yourself." - A Course in Miracles

IN THE PHYSICAL WORLD, an idol is anyone or anything you see as the source of your good - whether it is a mate, a job, money, success, a healthy body, an attractive face, skills and talents, a relationship, a house, a retirement plan, a church or guru, your children or family. All of these people, places and things are neutral. Their value is set by whatever part of the mind is focused on them at the moment - the right mind, or the insane wrong mind.

The only partner you will ever need is God within you. When you think of another mortal being as your partner, whether as a mate or in business, you have set that person up for a horrible fall and made them the object of the ego's attack thoughts and projections. You have put them in a prison of your own making where you also must dwell in order to keep an eye on them at all times. This IS suffering of your own design and it brings tremendous stress to everyone involved. The only path to peace is by keeping your eyes on God, and on your own paper. Release everyone and everything. They are only the vessels through which Spirit operates, they are not the Source.

If you are waiting for someone else to get their act together or to DO SOMETHING, you have taken a hostage and you are in hell. Husbands and wives are not to be "providers" for one another, nor to be co-conspirators in keeping the dangerous world from closing in. Spirit is the only true Provider for you who want the peace and joy of God. Spouses are not to be "partners" in keeping a house running and the bills paid - for YOU, God is that partner and your spouse is simply another child of God under the same roof, making the journey home together. We understand this is a very advanced lesson. Remember, the more advanced the lesson, the more simple and childlike the mind of the student must be.

Your task is to work on JOYFUL trust in God rather than hesitant fearful trust. Give the vessels in your life gratitude, praise and honor, but do not make them sources and do not put your trust in them - not because they are not trustworthy but because they are not your Source.

> *"Put all your faith in the Love of*
> *God within you; eternal, changeless*
> *and forever unfailing.*
> *This is the answer to whatever*
> *confronts you today."*
> *–A Course in Miracles*

Notice the word "ALL" in the quote above. Once again, it is time to free ALL the hostages whom you have made the source of your peace and good, or the source of your suffering and stress. It is time to remember Who you are and

Whose you are. This will bring the peace, joy and good that is yours by Divine Inheritance. BE HAPPY about this and you will find that you look at the people, places and things in your life with eyes of gentle loving innocence once again. This release has not left you on your own but instead had left you with the only Partner who never fails, never falters. BREATHE IN THIS PEACE NOW as you unclench your jaw, drop the shoulders, relax the body, and sink down into the One Presence in which every need is met; remembering that in God all is truly well and only Love is real.

And now, if you have any need, turn to Spirit within rather than to worldly vessels. Speak directly to Source as you open to receive whatever it is you have need of; whatever is the desire of your heart. Do not give a sales pitch. You are not trying to convince a worldly parent that you "deserve" a present or reward. The Divine Parent is your own true Self, not a thing apart from you with separate desires and needs. In God, there is no ego to be satisfied with flattery and religious practices. At the same time, hold nothing back from Source - keep no separate areas "for yourself" as you often do in mortal partnerships. Offer everything, give everything, keep no secrets and no secret stash or you are once again beginning to build an idol and a separate kingdom.

At last, this is the one Partnership which can offer the joy and serenity that you seek.

69. Dwell on LIFE!

"The journey to the cross should be the last "useless journey." Do not dwell upon it, but dismiss it as accomplished. If you can accept it as your own last useless journey, you are also free to join my resurrection. Until you do so your life is indeed wasted." - A Course in Miracles

PLEASE REMEMBER it is A Course in Miracles, not A Course in Crisis Management. Even for far too many "spiritual-type" mortals, God is the refuge of the needy and wounded only. This is akin to thinking that yoga, biking, walking, hiking and gyms are only for the morbidly obese rather ways of expanding the joy and aliveness of ALL beings who choose to do them.

The life of Spirit is not merely the answer to misery, it is the path to ever greater expanding JOY, peace, love and harmony for those who are already happy, joyous and free. It is for ALL, not only for the survivors, but for the THRIVERS as well! Still, humans are quite often unconsciously addicted to cheap drama, chaos, suffering, pain and all the worldly forms of crucifixion. Remember, the first goal that peace must flow over in order for you to see it is YOUR DESIRE TO GET RID OF IT. There is a human tendency to not trust the good in life, while immediately believing the very worst without the slightest hesitation.

THIS is the turn-around We are here to Help you with each day. It is your task to DWELL not on crucifixion but on resurrection and LIFE - and not just in times of crisis, but every day AS a way of life. We want you to begin to SAVOR and MILK the good - to suck the juice out of each day by focusing on the good in every person, every situation, every happening big or small. It is entirely up to you whether you will make the best of things, or the worst of things. No one else is thinking in your head, but since like attracts like, each thought you focus on invites more like thoughts into your mind. You were not born to come fix a broken world, nor to fix a supposed tear in the Universe. THAT IS THE USELESS HOPELESS JOURNEY.

You came to DEMONSTRATE peace by BEING

peaceful, to demonstrate LOVE BY BEING LOVE, to DEMONSTATE JOY by BEING JOYFUL. You cannot give what you do not have. The TOMB IS EMPTY so get the hell out of there and get out into the sunshine where LIFE awaits you today. We have much to JOYFULLY accomplish together!

70. Do You

"Again, - nothing you do or think or wish or make is necessary to establish your worth." - A Course in Miracles

YOU ARE NO SURPRISE TO GOD. Trying to be some idealized version of what you think is an acceptable or more "spiritual" self is a waste of your precious energy and time. Trying to force yourself into some new way of being is frustrating, time consuming and usually leads to failure and depression. You have a unique role to fulfill in the plan for salvation - if you go around trying to be somebody else, who will fill YOUR right place?

Certainly there are parts of your personality that We are working on. Let US. Do not try to change yourself, but instead surrender to His Grace every day and simply practice greater WILLINGNESS. What you try to "fix" usually ends up increasing or retreating only to come up with more virulence in some other form. We will lead you each day to the people, situations, books, teachers, and lessons that can best support you in gently releasing any old false ideas or behaviors which no longer serve your greater Self.

Your path is YOUR path. All beings are the many colored threads in the master tapestry. Each one is unique and yet all are One in God. It is not enough that you give up any harsh or critical thinking about other people; you must include yourself when you decide each day to release the hostages. Who you are is an individualized expression of the One Life. Honor and respect that as more than good enough to do what is given you to do.

Endlessly second-guessing yourself and allowing self doubt to crucify you only delays the miracles planned for you IN THE PRESENT moment. We have need for a YOU today, just as you are and just as you are not. Soften into this awareness and allow the day to unfold in perfect Order as we line up all that is needed to have a day in which Divine Appointment after Divine Appointment is met with Grace, joy and ease.

71. Daily Curriculum

"The Holy Spirit needs a happy learner, in whom His mission can be happily accomplished. You who are steadfastly devoted to misery must first recognize that you are miserable and not happy." - A Course in Miracles

REMEMBER AGAIN THAT THE FIRST OBSTACLE that peace must flow over in order for you to feel it is, the desire to get rid of it. We feel We must keep reminding you of this. It may sound harsh, but it is true just the same, that many humans are so devoted to their own misery that it actually gives them a perverse kind of happiness to BE as miserable as possible. Many are actually repelled by the concepts of JOY, peace, abundance, health, deep rest, savoring the good, making the best of things and simply ENJOYING daily life exactly as it is.

Lessons can be joyful or misery-inducing depending on the kind of student you choose to be. It is the attitude of the student more than the lesson that really determines how everything goes forward. Just the same, choose your teacher carefully. An unhappy teacher teaches unhappiness. A peaceful teacher teaches peace. This is because to teach is to demonstrate and teaching is not accomplished through words but rather through Consciousness. Words CAN be helpful, but they can also be confusing and confounding for they are but "*symbols of symbols*" and are not the thing itself. They are the finger pointing at the moon, not the moon itself. Consciousness is the thing - and you can feel and sense Consciousness if you will quiet your mind.

The ego can even twist the words of the Course in order to increase suffering rather than releasing you from it if you are not vigilant for the peace of God within you. Much religious thinking is like this - focusing on false dogma about deprivation, sacrifice, self loathing, not getting too happy, staying limited. And this error is the result of allowing ego to steal your joy again. The ego's lessons are harsh, hard, sharp and critical. The Holy Spirit's lessons are gently planned by One Who cares for you and knows the way out of suffering quickly. Choose your teacher carefully each morning as you begin your day.

> *"The opposite of joy is depression. When your learning promotes depression instead of joy, you cannot be listening to God's joyous Teacher and learning His lessons."*
> —A Course in Miracles

Together with the Holy Spirit today, it is your task to find things to be happy about - to take charge of promoting joy within yourself rather than misery. Again, it is entirely up to you how you tell the story of your day, or of your life. You can make the best of it, or you can make the worst of it. You can choose gentle kind downstream thoughts, or you can fight against the current and choose to struggle your way upstream. Which seems like the "*better choice*" to you?

72. Divine Opportunity Knocks

"Confidence cannot develop fully until mastery has been accomplished. We have already attempted to correct the fundamental error that fear can be mastered, and have emphasized that the only real mastery is through love. Readiness is only the beginning of confidence. You may think this implies that an enormous amount of time is necessary between readiness and mastery, but let me remind you that time and space are under my control."
- A Course in Miracles

IT IS TRUE that opportunity only knocks once - once every moment. There it is again, there is it again, there is it again. We are not saying this so that you will become so complacent that you never bother to answer the knock at the door, but rather to help you heal any sense of regret over having gotten to the door seemingly "too late." There is no such thing as too late in God; not within this "no fault" Universe. And the reason it is a "no fault" Universe is because YOU are an eternal spirit being with endless opportunities to keep making the better choice.

HOWEVER, miracles are a means of saving time so that there is much more time for having fun, savoring and enjoying the opportunities that have been taken. Your part is not to create the opportunities - not even to "attract" them to you. Your part is to be calmly present and awake when they arrive. Your part is to be prepared.

How to prepare? Simple, spend as much time as possible marinating in the One Divine Presence. We don't mean sitting off somewhere on a meditation cushion in total silence (although that may be part of it). Rather, We mean no matter where you are or what is happening around you at the time you can remain in the God-Zone. It is an AWARENESS of the Presence even in the midst of a traffic jam or while picking up the dog poop. It may be as simple as the thought "God, God, God" or "Peace, Peace, Peace" as you go through your daily routine.

As you "*practice the Presence*" more and more, you will develop the confidence the Course is talking about. When Divine Opportunity knocks you will not feel full of anxiety and extreme adrenaline, but will feel a magnificent calm delight instead. This confidence is not in your limited human self, but in the Self that God created. It is truly effortless to be Who and What you really are. This is not to say that you will not be busy. You may be busier than ever before, but it will be a busyness that is absent of STRUGGLE. Only the ego struggles. Spirit is forever in the State of Grace. Therefore, relate to Spirit rather than ego and automatically your confidence begins to rise. This is mastery through Love. And as you learn to become a Master of Love, you can even begin to receive "*double for your trouble,*" which is a means of accepting all the blessings that you passed by along the way. They have been held in trust for you until you develop the Consciousness to receive them.

Many Divine Opportunities are planned for you this very day. Simply be calm and prepared by spending as much time as possible in awareness of your Infinite Source, the One Divine Presence within you. We are here. We are ready. We will Help if you ask and allow.

73. *Pour Forth the Oil*

"You can wait, delay, paralyze yourself, or reduce your creativity almost to nothing. But you cannot abolish it." - A Course in Miracles

Like your Divine Parent, you are a born creator. It is your nature to be creative, and creators create. When you are not creating, you will tend to feel less joyful and less alive because you are denying who and what you are. And that in itself is a key point - create from JOY and to stimulate JOY rather than to try to achieve, accomplish or get something. All of that frequently happens when you create, but it is not the point. Create because it is your Divine Destiny to do so.

Writers write. Lovers love. Mothers mother. Painters paint. Singers sing. Farmers farm. Teachers teach. Runners run. Researchers research. And each of you have a multitude of roles to play. You must keep pouring forth creativity from within, FOR YOUR OWN SAKE, because it is an expression of the One Life, the One Mind, AS YOU. The only reason you sometimes lack joy in this is because you have allowed the ego thought system to pervert this process with myths about competition, finite resources, getting something out of it, SELLING, bartering, marketing, branding, forcing, sacrificing, schedules, worldly expectations, suffering and a whole litany of lies used to terrify you into creative paralysis. DO NOT LET EGO STEAL YOUR JOY! JOY is the attracting factor in your life.

Go back to the well again every day to draw from the Infinite SOURCE of all creativity and drink from the

JOYOUS Living Waters. Then, when you come back to the world, begin to pour forth from within you whatever is your daily portion - GIVE IT OUT from within you freely and joyfully. Creators create whether anyone is noticing, paying attention, giving praise, paying or not. It is your nature to bring forth what is within you whether the world notices or not. And the more you do this, the happier you will become.

"For this is what the Lord, the God of Israel, says: 'The jar of flour will not be used up and the jug of oil will not run dry until the day the Lord sends rain on the land.'

She went away and did as Elijah had told her. So there was food every day for Elijah and for the woman and her family. For the jar of flour was not used up and the jug of oil did not run dry, in keeping with the word of the Lord spoken by Elijah." – 1 Kings, 17: 14-16

Each day you must pour forth what you can because YOU ARE a Creator, and you must create from what is within you. You MUST LET IT OUT, you must prime the pump. And the more you pour forth, the more there will be. As a Creator, you do not deplete your resources - in fact, what you do not use, you tend to lose - but never all of it. You can reduce it almost to nothing, but you cannot abolish it. When you have creatively seemed to run dry, it is almost always because you have forgotten about the JOY and have become distracted by calendars, clocks, contracts, deadlines, finances, chores, reputation and the thousands of ego distraction that tell you who you are NOT instead of who you ARE.

Each day is your own unique co-creation with the Life in you and around you. What will you pour forth today from this JOYOUS Source?

74. The Peace of God

"I want the peace of God. To say these words is nothing. But to mean these words is everything. If you could but mean them for just an instant, there would be no further sorrow possible for you in any form; in any place or time. Heaven would be completely given back to full awareness, memory of God entirely restored, the resurrection of all creation fully recognized. No one can mean these words and not be healed." - A Course in Miracles

THE PEACE THE WORLD GIVES is ephemeral at best. It is the seeming peace of *"I have a refuge from the storms of life because I am loved in a special way by a spouse or child, my family is okay, our bills are paid, we have money saved, we are healthy and work is plentiful."* This is not peace at all but rather a kind of temporary release from tension. They are certainly things to savor and enjoy, but they are no replacement for the Peace of God.

The Peace of God passes ALL understanding simply because it does not evaporate in the heat of stressful times, it does not wash away in the storms of life. It literally makes no sense at all to the ego mind. It is the peace that the mortals around you cannot understand if they have not surrendered to this Peace. And this Peace is the kind that can ONLY come from a total surrender and letting go. This is the Peace that comes by ending the war, when you have waved the white flag and given yourself over totally to the Greater Power. You have stopped trusting in your own puny little strength. You have laid aside your strategies and defenses, your sword and your shield. You are no longer motivated and hyped up to go into battle yet another day.

Now the softening has come. Now the space for miracles has been made and the way is clear at last. Where once there was fear and a desperate neediness, there is now a willingness to let all things be exactly as they are, knowing that whatever the present trial, this too shall pass, as every storm does. There has never been a night which did not end in the rising of the sun. Never been a winter that has not melted into spring. This is a most happy and joyous defeat! There is no shame at all in this kind of surrender for it is the victory of defeat! Be glad that your way has failed for it was a way of endless thinking, thinking, thinking in which there is very little true peace or respite.

Now we return to the gentle paths in which the Peace within you is not disturbed by the endless physical winds of change in external circumstances. BREATHE IN THE GRACE OF GOD NOW as you RELEASE and LET GO of strategies and defenses. Rest in God and LISTEN for the still small voice. This is less a time of prayer and more a time of stillness. Too many of your prayers are merely an endless chattering to Source in an effort to get your "needs" met. God knows your needs before you do. It is time to be quiet. It is time at last to LISTEN to wisdom from a Thought System beyond your own. God is on the Field - and God has GOT this if only you will take your hands off it long enough to let the Peace of God within you rise up and take over. This is that time. Do not go numb, or to sleep, but stay awake within the Peace of God where you receive, rather than get - where you are slowly fed what truly nourishes instead of gobbling down that which only leaves you more ravenous. BE STILL within, even while you are making your phone calls, taking your steps, doing your work. At all times there can be a part of your Consciousness which is saying,

> *"Speak Lord, I am listening for Your Word and Guidance today. And above all else, I want the Peace of God. Make joyful use of me today."*

SLOW DOWN - BREATHE - RELAX - LET GO

75. Go For the Feeling

"Let us not forget, however, that words are but symbols of symbols. They are thus twice removed from reality." - A Course in Miracles

THIS COURSE IS MADE UP OF WORDS, but too often you allow your semantics to confound and confuse away you from the real purpose of the Course itself. It is the triumph of the ego that so many have ended up fighting over the words, or becoming depressed by them. Again, do not let the ego steal your joy. The only purpose of the words is to lead you to the experience of God's eternal Peace within you. An intellectual understanding without the experience of Peace is just another way of increasing suffering and fear.

There are only two thought systems, one feels good and one feels bad. This is as simple as We can make it for you. How you feel is your sign of which thought system you are currently activating within yourself. If you do not like how you feel, change to the better thought system. This is the gift of contrast in your world. But remember, We are talking about the good feeling of PEACE, not simply relief. The ego wants relief, but your soul craves God's Peace. Your ego may feel relief by telling someone off, by making that person get off your back, by expressing some rage or by "venting" endlessly over some old wound. But inside, you know that this is not Peace, and therefore it does not really satisfy or last.

The Peace of God does not come from getting rid of some unpleasant or uncomfortable feeling. Peace is the result of no longer justifying or defending whatever attack thoughts have arisen in your mind - and by surrendering them to the Holy Spirit with no shame or blame as you then begin to choose the better thought system.

CHOOSE how you want to FEEL today. Be deliberate in this. Then, remind yourself frequently that there are only two thought systems, one feels good, and one feels bad. Keep making the better choice as you go and let miracles replace all grievances.

76. All Things Are Possible

"And let us rejoice that there is an answer to what seems to be a conflict with no resolution possible. All things are possible to God." - A Course in Miracles

WITHIN THE ILLUSION OF TIME, it is sad just how many miracles you manage to talk yourselves out of by being "reasonable" or by handling everything on your own. Along with that, there is a tendency to flip into the "control mode" as soon as anything frightens you, and this often either makes things worse, or inhibits the natural unfolding to something NEW and ultimately wonderful. Maintaining status quo in your lives is not really a miracle mindset. Sometimes the very thing you are desperately trying to hold onto is precisely the thing that's got to go in order for you to experience even greater good. The only control worth cultivating is self-control.

Mastery of self is more beneficial than trying to master that which seems to be outside of you.

This is why the development of trust is such an important part of your spiritual evolution. This can be something as simple as reminding yourself throughout the day, *"God is with me now. With God, ALL things are possible for me."* We want you to begin using your imagination in more positive ways instead of using it to worry and fret. Within the Possibility Matrix, all things are possible. THE POSSIBILITY MATRIX IS A COSMIC GRID OF DYNAMIC ENERGY. It is the place that gives structure to your dreams or to your nightmares.

It may surprise you that it is not really your thoughts that are most important or powerful within the Matrix, but rather your emotional energy. Because of this, it is not even all that important that you think of or envision any particular scenario. In fact, many of you find the idea of visualizing or thinking creatively so stressful that you are actually misusing the Matrix. It is far more important that you practice FEELING relaxed, peaceful and JOYOUS - and this requires TRUST and letting go of the preoccupation with strategies, plans, defenses and schemes. It is not a place of grabbing hold of your dreams, but rather of letting go of the emotional habits which block them. The Matrix Itself then is a place of relaxed joyous SURRENDER to the Peace of God.

You might think that you need to enter the Matrix and think specifically of what you would like to have happen in your life - but really, you could just as easily enter the Matrix and think of puppies running in fields of flowers and if that image stimulates a relaxed delightful joy in you, it would open your energy centers to a greater good than most specific visualizing does. Just for now, practice FEELING GOOD within the Possibility Matrix for short periods of time throughout the day. All you need do at this point to begin practice is take 3 deep cleansing breaths, relax the body, and imagine yourself floating up into the Upper Room of Consciousness as you align with Source. In this space, let go of the concept that God is with you, and move even deeper into the realization,

> *"God and I are ONE. All seeming barriers and separation are now dissolving as I melt into the Joy and Peace of the Infinite Presence."*

And even if you only spend one minute there, you will have done more to allow greater possibilities than if you'd done 20 minutes of affirmations. Then, when you come back to your 3 dimensional world awareness, do not allow yourself to return to the control or worry modes. Instead, TRUST your intuition and Guidance to take you through whatever the day brings. We ARE ever with you and are as useful as your willingness will allow Us to be.

All things are possible with God and miracles are a means of saving time.

77. Qi Surfing

"Listen – perhaps you catch a hint of an ancient state not quite forgotten; dim, perhaps, and yet not altogether unfamiliar, like a song whose name is long forgotten, and the circumstances in which you heard completely unremembered . . . But you remember, from just this little part, how lovely was the song, how wonderful the setting where you heart it, and how you

loved those who were there and listened with you." – A Course in Miracles

ENERGY IS RISING AND FALLING ALL THE TIME. There is a time and a season to everything. Everything is energy or Qi. Learn to pay attention to the Energy present at any given time, in any given place, including within yourself. Energy waves are much like the waves of the ocean. They have a natural flow and the tide goes in, and the tide goes out. Too often humans are trying to surf when the tide is out. Energetically, you may be trying to sow seeds when the ground is covered with winter snow, or you are trying to ski down a hill covered with lush grass.

SLOW DOWN and TUNE IN to the force of the Qi within and around you. You can learn to sense and feel the energy present. This is yet another miraculous means of saving time and energy. Remember the times when someone wanted to have a deep talk with you, or ask you to do them a favor at the exact wrong moment? Perhaps you were overwhelmed and in a very defensive mood right when they wanted to address some behavior of yours . . . didn't go very well, did it?

This is where your meditative practice can be of the most help. If you spend time each day quieting and focusing your mind, it helps you to be more tuned in to the Qi vibrations around you so that you are not trying to push a noodle up a hill all day long. With practice you will begin to know when it is time to run out into the Energetic Ocean ready to surf the gorgeous waves, and when it is time to go inside to rest while waiting out the low tide or the storm that is raging.

The more you learn to tune in to the subtle vibrations, the more you will also learn how to actually work with and influence those energies so that your own Consciousness will begin to call forth the Energies you want at any given time and place. Again, first SELF mastery, THEN mastery of conditions. Pay attention to your Qi today and learn to work with where it is right now, instead of thinking or judging that it should be otherwise. As you meet it where it is and begin to work with it in the present, you can learn to gradually move it through Conscious Intention rather than through bullying - a much better way to work with Energies. Don't try harder, try softer.

78. Softening

"You are not really capable of being tired, but you are very capable of wearying yourself. The strain of constant judgment is virtually intolerable. It is curious that an ability so debilitating would be so deeply cherished." - A Course in Miracles

EVERYTHING THAT YOU NEED IS ALREADY HERE, right now. It is only your weak ability to SEE which keeps you seeking after what has already been given. The ego mind is most often invalidating whatever is near, while idolizing what seems to be missing or far off. This keeps you in hell in your present. What if you simply chose not to judge your present for the next 24 hours? What if you decided to simply be present without a story of how anyone or anything should be different?

You may think that if you accepted all, including yourself, as is, that nothing would ever "improve" or get better. Actually, you would begin to SEE more clearly the gifts that you'd passed over before in your rush to judgment. In fact, you would learn to make positive changes through the inspiration of LOVE rather than through the motivation of fear. You would think less in terms of getting anything, and more in terms of sharing and contributing. It is a state in which the mind grows calm, and the heart opens. This is the opposite of the rigidity that the ego counsels you to.

It truly is exhausting and debilitating to endlessly judge and critique every single thing that is happening around you and in the world all day long as worthy or unworthy, wanted or unwanted, acceptable or unacceptable, right or wrong, good or bad. Miracles not only save time, they save energy by eliminating the mental stress and strain of policing the Universe.

Start by softening your heart today. Deliberately choose to give everyone and everything a day off from your evaluation, criticism and helpful hints. Let any changes you choose to make come from a place of LOVE and creating space for more love. You may make it as simple as asking the question, *"How can I express more love in this area of my life?"* Simple, simple, simple.

79. Infinite Good

"Because God's equal Sons have everything, they cannot compete. Yet if they perceive any of their brothers as anything other than their perfect equals, the idea of competition has entered their minds. Do not underestimate your need to be vigilant against this idea, because all conflicts come from it. It is the belief that conflicting interests are possible, and therefore you have accepted the impossible as true." - A Course in Miracles

THE EGO-DOMINATED WORLD is built on the illusion of competition and finite resources. It is the root of all war, whether between nations, companies or individuals. It is the father of all lies. In this case, the opposite of competition is cooperation. It is what neutralizes and dissolves the belief in separate interests and limited good. The Truth is, the more you cooperate and share, the more good is brought forth and created for all concerned.

You live in a time in which this illusion of competition has never been stronger. An enormous amount of your TV shows are "game shows" and competition shows where everyone is scrambling over each other, often with bitterness and despair, at the other "competitors" in order to get the ONE and only prize available. This is so much darker than you can imagine and what it does to your psyche and subconscious is what is costing you the peace you say you want. Nice guys don't finish last - nice guys aren't racing - they are running for the PURE JOY of the running itself.

When the Course says, *"To have, give all, to all"* what do you think it means? It does not mean to give away all your "stuff" or money and keep nothing for yourself. It is the remembrance that there is no lack of good for YOU if you will renounce the idea of limitation and scarcity. There is always enough if you could only change your mind - enough money, enough jobs, enough homes, enough energy, enough good ideas, enough help, enough friends and mates, enough opportunities, enough resources, enough time, enough love, enough chances . . . but what you BELIEVE, YOU invoke and call forth. The world you SEE is the one YOU believe in, even if you hate and fear it.

There IS another way. It begins with a shift in thinking AWAY from competition and toward cooperation. There are teachers and even business leaders in your world right now who are pointing the way toward the New Paradigm in which the children of God soothe, uplift, inspire, cooperate and share with one another as a way to the GREATEST wealth and success in ALL areas of life. And as you help a sister or brother realize their dreams, your own dreams are brought closer than ever before. *"Do onto others"* is actually a spiritual formula for creating the miracles YOU yourself want to experience.

Remember frequently today that you are living in an Infinite Universe with Infinite Good that is never depleted in any way. It is the IDEA of limitation that MAKES the limitations you "see." There is no need to race against anyone else and if you like the idea of "beating" someone, then simply work to beat your own old record of ALLOWING greater good than you have before. No one is ever stopping you but you and a stressful story you tell yourself. Tell a happy story today dear Miracle Worker and see how easily things unfold for you and all those around you who choose the path of greater allowing. In time, it will seem to you as though the good and resources are chasing you down!

80. *There Is No Death*

"There is no death. The Son of God is free." - A Course in Miracles

NOTHING IN YOUR WORLD is as shrouded in superstitious ideas as that of the illusion you call death. In Truth, death is nothing more than a shifting of attention, a difference in vibrational rate. When this shift is made, the illusion of the body drops and disintegrates. It is not even a release, for it is only thought that ever imprisons. The body does not imprison at all, but the story mind tells can make a prison of anything.

The Truth is, you are free NOW if you choose to SEE the Truth. The body is not inhibiting your experience unless you use it for that purpose. A body is nothing more than a means of communication with others who also believe they are bodies. Yet many of you treat your cell phone with more care and attention than you do the body. Additionally, you have all kinds of intense emotions and stories about it - you ignore it, judge it, fear it, worry about it, focus on it too much, abuse it, trash it, worship it, and obsess about the future of it . . . such a waste of energy and time.

If you would think of it the way you do a cell phone you would be much better off. Keep it clean, the screen clear, charged with energy, connected to Source, with up-to-date Software downloaded from Source, and let it rest in the charger overnight. Just do this and see how much more ease and peace you have with it.

Then, when "death" comes, you realize that your account has not been cancelled, you're merely being upgraded to a Higher Communication Carrier in which the receiving and transmitting equipment is so much lighter and elegant in design that those with the old equipment cannot even see you. YOU have not changed nor been set free, you've merely upgraded your instrument of communication for something with far less technical glitches or limitations. Life goes on. It always has. It always will. There is no end to you nor anyone you have even known or will know. There are no dropped calls ever, only a tendency to hang up too soon while blaming the equipment. Treat the body with kindness no matter what it is going through. Remember, that the simplest most elegant philosophy of life is just that, be kind.

81. Mind and Matter

"Projection makes perception. The world you see is what you gave it, nothing more than that. But though it is no more than that, it is not less. Therefore, to you it is important. It is the witness to your state of mind, the outside picture of an inward condition. As a man thinketh, so does he perceive. Therefore, seek not to change the world, but choose to change your mind about the world. Projection is a result and not a cause. And that is why order of difficulty in miracles is meaningless. Everything looked upon with vision is healed and holy." - A Course in Miracles

FAR TOO MANY SPIRITUAL PRACTITIONERS still think of "mind over matter" as a kind of quaint parlor trick of a bygone era, or as a remnant of hypnotists and those who mesmerize. It is treated as an exception to the rational laws of the world. It is not exception at all, it IS Law. Mind and matter are one.

There is no objective world at all. There is only YOUR world, and that world is made up of your stories, beliefs, attitudes and projections. Change these, and what you observe will change along with them. Perception is cause, not a result. This is difficult for humans to understand because it is so totally rejected from the very start. Yet, with patient practice, you can begin to see that it is indeed quite true. The world you see, is the one you make every day through what you choose to believe and focus upon. There are no "lucky" people, only people who perceive differently.

Today, you can practice creating your world joyfully or stressfully. It begins right where you are, as you are, in this moment. We begin by simply reaching for slightly better feeling thoughts. The goal is not to go from worry to bliss in 10 seconds. The jump is too far to make and this is why so many try this path and then abandon it as another "fantasy" of false hope. Going from first grade to graduate school is a grave error leading to feelings of failure and depression.

The easiest way of all to begin is with a simple practice of gratitude and appreciation throughout the day. Look for things to appreciate in YOUR world, and you are already beginning to shape your world. Another excellent practice is to regularly say or make lists which begin with the phrase, *"You know what I love . . . ."* And then you begin filling in with as many things as you can think of . . . *I love it when the dog comes running to greet me at the door, I love it when there is a parking space right in front, I love these clear blue sky mornings, I love a new journal, I love listening to my meditation music, I love reading at lunch, I love it when the coffee is just the right temperature like this, I love the smell of my baby's head after a bath, I love the comfy throw on the sofa while I'm napping, I love when I am able to accomplish a lot at work in the mornings, I love when the traffic just disappears ahead of me from out of nowhere* . . . and on and on and on.

All of this, IS creating YOUR world for you. And Consciousness animates matter. YOUR world is responding to YOUR thoughts. Begin to look for the evidence of good, and good is what you will find. Look for the evidence of love, and love is what you will find. Begin to look for the evidence of prosperity, and prosperity is what you will find. ENJOY the process and RELAX into it. Do not get tense or overly excited. Cultivate an attitude of CALM DELIGHT as you watch YOUR world of joyful ease come into focus ever more clearly each and every day.

82. *True Relaxation*

"Relax for the rest of the practice period, confident that your efforts, however meager, are fully supported by the strength of God and all His Thoughts. It is from Them that your strength will come." - A Course in Miracles

WE WANT YOU TO EXPAND your concept of what it means "to relax" in your world. Far too often you tend to think of it as sleep, or being flopped onto the sofa like a rag doll, or as something that happens in a spa when you are far from your normal life. These are but very limited ideas of what true relaxation is and this perceived limitation keeps you from understanding how available it is at all times and in all places.

Relaxation is not a deadening of the senses but rather a state in which the mind can be alert yet perfectly calm. This is a very attractive state of Consciousness for good. <u>What We are really advocating here is a RELAXED JOY</u>. It is not passive so much as it is a calm expectancy of good.

Do you know that you can be perfectly relaxed while looking for a new job, auditioning for the part, writing the book, preparing a dinner party, negotiating the loan, making the sales pitch, going on a first date, giving the speech . . . all of it. This relaxation is not a lack of caring or passion, but it is a lack of tension and fear. This kind of relaxation does not put you to sleep so much as it opens the door to take **inspired aligned action**. From this state of being you are much more in touch and in alignment with the Guidance within you. It is much easier to hear the Voice for God when you are relaxed than when you are tense and afraid.

Ask for Guidance and then relax and <u>EXPECT an answer</u>. This is not something that is limited to being on your meditation mat in a "spiritual" setting but is just as possible in the middle of an amusement park surrounded by 10,000 people rushing about you in a frenzy. Remember that God goes with you wherever you go because God is in your mind. Rest in this awareness at all times and practice sensing that connection at all places, all times, under all circumstances. Breathe it in as you relax your jaw and tongue, drop your shoulders, feel all the muscles of your skull loosen and relax and allow the Light to pour down through the top of your head, flooding your entire being with a golden glow of Peace and Joy.

The Thoughts of God will carry your through this day as you walk through the open doors to your greater good.

83. Believe It In

"The great poet, the late Robert Frost said, 'Our founding fathers did not believe in the future, they believed it in.' They didn't think about bringing about democracy; that time would bring about the country you and I love and live in today; they believed it in." - Neville Goddard

THROUGH THE POSSIBILITY MATRIX, or Christ Consciousness, you "believe" your entire world into existence for you. We don't mean the "Earth" in which you all seem to dwell, but the individual world YOU are living in today. It is unique to you. There is no objective world "out there." Each sees her own world, the one she "believed-in" through attitudes, thoughts, perceptions, actions, and expectations.

Every conversation and magazine article you read is *"believing-in"* YOUR particular world. Therefore, it should matter quite a lot to you what you give your attention to each moment of every day. There are no neutral thoughts. All are creative, which is not to say that each of them physically manifests. There is no need to fear your negative thoughts or to get superstitious about thinking. It takes a lot of chewing on a particular negative thought vibration for it to manifest in the physical. Positive thoughts actually manifest in the physical much more quickly and effortlessly because they are more in alignment with Reality as God created It.

You may be surprised at just how quickly a negative spiral can dissipate and be turned around into an upward and gentle floating toward the Light. The hard part is how attracted and attached humans are to drama, pain, struggle and stories. It's time to let that go poodle. We know you are growing weary of that path. Let Us help you dissolve all those old patterns by simply turning away from the old and turning toward the NEW. We start here and now - what is the day you choose to believe in for yourself? Take a moment right now to right it down. How do you want to FEEL today? What do you want your dominant attitude to be? How open are you to receive? CHOOSE it now, and the way to believe it in is to start by BELIEVING that it is possible for you through the Power and Presence of the Possibility Matrix within you.

84. We Are Here

"My control can take over everything that does not matter, while my guidance can direct everything that does, if you so choose." - A Course in Miracles

You still spend too much time going it alone - quite needlessly.

We see how you are trying and We also see the wonderful steps forward you are making. But We could still be making it even easier for you if you would allow it - and the way you allow it is by thinking of the Christ Within you frequently throughout the day.

Pushing through and rushing forward is not the way to greatest achievement, as you must know by now. It is through Divine Collaboration that greatest strides forward are made. We can handle your day. We can easily rearrange time and space for your greatest good, peace, ease and joy. We can help you with the meaningless minutiae and with the truly important, and We are much more aware of the true difference between the two.

Lean on Us today miracle worker. You deserve the peace and joy of God even as you go about your most "unspiritual" of tasks today. We want you to accomplish all you would like today, but without the cracking of the whip, without the worry, without any fear. You are so very precious to Us in every way and you do not allow Us to show it as much as We would dearly love to.

Whatever seems too much for you today, give it to Us. Whatever you may resist or dread, give it to Us. Whatever you cannot figure out, give it to Us. Whatever it may seem difficult or even impossible to get through today, give it to Us. Whatever bores you, or you would rather not do, give it to Us. We are here FOR YOU.

85. A Campaign of Innocence

"You undertook, together, to invite the Holy Spirit into your relationship. He could not have entered otherwise. Although you may have made many

mistakes since then, you have also made enormous efforts to help Him do His work. And He has not been lacking in appreciation for all you have done for Him. Nor does He see the mistakes at all. Have you been similarly grateful to your brother? Have you consistently appreciated the good efforts, and overlooked mistakes? Or has your appreciation flickered and grown dim in what seemed to be the light of the mistakes? Perhaps you are now entering upon a campaign to blame him for the discomfort of the situation in which you find yourself. And by this lack of thanks and gratitude you make yourself unable to express the holy instant, and thus lose sight of it." - A Course in Miracles

OH YES DEAR ONES, We do understand the temptation to categorize and detail the errors of all those who are falling short of your ideals for them, and for all living beings. But what you may not realize is that since your thoughts never leave your own mind, it is YOU who is being MOST hurt by this meticulous record keeping. Nothing is ever "gotten rid of" by projecting it outward because the faulty movie and projector are IN YOU, where they remain.

The only real happy option is to show a different movie altogether. <u>Humans say that they will forgive but never forget, and this is the fundamental error We want you to understand. Your world is totally opposite to Truth</u>. You think that if you forget the past you are doomed to repeat it, but in fact, it is in the constant focus on the hurts and errors of the past that YOUR world is destined to keep repeating the pattern in the present. This is no less radical now than when Brother Jesus taught it a few thousands of your years ago - in fact, it is MORE disturbing to the ego mind now than it was then. Truth is very disturbing to the mind that refuses to heal.

DO NOT RUMINATE ON A PAINFUL PAST IN REMEMBRANCE OF WHAT YOU THINK WAS LOST. The story of Lot's wife in one of the human scriptures is there to let you know that turning around to see the destruction of the past only hardens you into what can be easily broken and crushed. The Miracle happens in the NOW. And as the Divine Presence is NOT keeping a record of your wrongs, it is clearly ironic that YOU would keep a record of anyone's mistakes, including your own. As Source has been grateful to you even through all of your errors, you would do well to do the same for others - not to be spiritual but because it feels GOOD to think as God does.

Focus instead on whatever things are good, whatever things are true, whatever things are lovely. Think on these things and free YOUR world from the relentless repeating of old wounds. Choose now to catalog the gifts, strengths, contributions, talents, and efforts of your partners in this life. See one another with KINDNESS and gentleness - add in a huge sense of humor as you take things more lightly and less personally. Find and focus on the positive aspects of YOUR world and amplify them as often as possible remembering that every word you speak and every thought you think is an affirmation. NEVER affirm that which you yourself would not wish to experience. Even with all your learning and growth, you still have only the very slightest inkling of just how much Power is available to you - the Power that creates worlds awaits the instruction of your thought in each moment.

You are designing your day - you are the architect - you are the programmer. Run the program that brings more of what you want to experience. There is no need to waste one moment of energy trying to delete the programs you don't want. All you need do is not run them anymore. They sit there on your desktop, but YOU are the one who activates them through the words you speak, the thoughts you think, the "casual" conversation you get into, and the things you focus on. Activate a PRESENT joy and let past stay in the past.

> *"The one true and holy thing you can say about the past is that it is not here."* - A Course in Miracles

86. *Listen, Learn and DO*

"There is no more self-contradictory concept than that of "idle thoughts." What gives rise to the perception of a whole world can hardly be called idle. EVERY thought you have contributes to truth or to illusion; either it extends truth or it multiplies illusions." - A Course in Miracles

ALL TOO FREQUENTLY miracle workers are writing with the right hand and then using their left hand to erasing what they've just written. This is what happens when you spend your morning doing your positive affirmations and setting the tone of your day, and then shortly thereafter begin making "jokes" and having "casual conversation" that is neutralizing all the things you spent the morning affirming. Or perhaps you are one who spends your precious Consciousness posting disturbing news on your internet pages thinking that you are Paul Revere, when in fact you are actually more like Chicken Little. There is no such thing as casual conversation. All thought creates form at some level.

Some of the most negative and detrimental vibrations you activate are around the concept of "hope." Hope is mostly just the path leading eventually to disappointment and hopelessness. Hope is for those who have NO faith, no belief, no real commitment to Truth. It is the faithless "casual conversation" in which you use the INCREDIBLE POWER

OF YOUR WORD AND THOUGHT to say things like, *"Yeah, I hope it works out."* Hope means you've relinquished real power to the ego again. Hope is the opposite of expecting.

NEVER speak anything you would not want to LIVE. EVERY word you ever use to describe your "self" is LITERALLY creating that very self in your now. Self-deprecation is not humility, it is the arrogant self-obsession of the ego running rampant - it literally depreciates the self and reminds you of who you are NOT instead of who you are. It is the erasing of the very life you pretend you want for yourself. Then you think, *"Oh, this stuff doesn't work. It's just a bunch of positive mumbo-jumbo and magical thinking"* when the truth is that it IS working FOR YOU by demonstrating that HOPING and lazy speaking is keeping you exactly where you've always been no matter how many books you've read or how many decades of seminars you attend. It is *"LISTEN, LEARN AND DO!"*

Remember, you are who YOU say you are and you live the life YOU narrate in your own mind. If you keep saying that it's HARD to do this, then **YOU ARE AFFIRMING THAT IT IS HARD FOR YOU AND YOUR WORD IS LAW UNTO YOUR LIFE**. If you begin to say, *"I am enjoying making positive changes in my life and in my Consciousness and it is FUN!"* then **BY THE LAW OF YOUR WORD THAT IS EXACTLY WHAT WILL BE YOUR EXPERIENCE AND THE TRUTH FOR YOU.**

Do not let the ego steal your joy today just because you think your negativity is cute and funny. Is it funny to never live the joyful life you could be living? Is that hilarious? Have you not noticed that your comedians who talk the most about how horrible the aging process is are the very ones who age most painfully and with the most health issues? Cause and effect, cause and effect, cause and effect. So simple.

87. *Let It Go, Let It Go, Let It Go*

"Yet the ego, though encouraging the search for love very actively, makes one proviso; do not find it. Its dictates, then, can be summed up simply as: 'Seek and do <u>not</u> find.'" – A Course in Miracles

THE ONLY WAY to experience real love is through radical defenselessness. It is not merely that in your defenselessness your safety lies, but also your peace, love, joy and your true Self are all found in the Consciousness of true defenselessness. In calling off the rabid search for what you want, you begin to gain miraculous access all that has already been given.

Right here, right now, is all that you need in order to experience the Peace and Love that passes all understanding. The tension and stress that arise from your defenses are what keep you from experiencing the overwhelming abundance which is already available to you in this very moment. "The Power of Now" is more than the title of yet another new age book to be read and quoted from - it is a reminder that there is NO power anywhere except in the now. Therefore, what is required is that you calm down and become PRESENT, open, defenselessness and available. This is an ACTIVE and ALERT relaxation, not a going to sleep nor laziness

To experience this power today, let go of your schemes and strategies. Let go of desperately trying to FIGURE OUT WHAT TO DO NEXT. Let go of resistance to where you currently are. Let go of stories about how people, places and situations "should be" - and let go of diagnosing the problems of the world as you let go of seeking who and what is to blame. RELAX into this Holy Instant and trust your inner Wisdom to lead you on the right path to your perfect expansion.

<u>We are with you. We've got this</u>. Stay connected and tuned in today and together We'll co-create a day of gentle sparkling miracles and Light.

88. Gentle Repentance

"For we know that the law is spiritual; but I am mortal, sold as a slave to sin (error/mistakes.) I do not understand what I do. For what I want to do, I do not do, but what I hate I do . . . For I have the desire to do what is good, but I cannot carry it out." - Romans 7:14

DEAREST URBAN MYSTIC, how wearying it is to live in self-condemnation simply because of your moments of backsliding down the mountain. There is no point in it at all because any ground that has been lost is much more quickly regained now - much more quickly than it took you to get this far, because now you know the way so much more clearly. Remember Our motto is "*progress, not perfection*." A perfect Practitioner is not of much help to those she is sent to Help because the vibrational variance would be far too great. We LOVE our imperfect Practitioners who are not afraid to admit to falling face first in the mud from time to time.

Remember, "repent" means turn around. When you are going in the wrong direction again, the answer is so very simple, turn around. Beating on your breast with guilt and shame, or looking into your past for someone to blame only delays the miracle of restoration. We know you disappoint yourself when you fall down - you were doing so well, and then seemingly from out of nowhere you are yelling at the kids or your spouse, overspending on the credit card, eating all the things you swore off of, sleeping through your first class, gossiping about your co-worker - and you feel like a spiritual failure. But it is not the mistake that is the enemy here but rather what ego does with the mistake after it's been made that steals your joy and robs you of the Peace of God.

<u>The Universe is ready to start over again RIGHT NOW, this very second</u>. The greatest delay in progress is rarely the mistake that was made, but rather how long you tend to hold onto it. And this is just as true when you are focusing on the guilt and mistakes in another person.

The Answer is to gently turn around and start again taking those penguin steps up the mountain. It is extremely rare that you have fallen as far as you THINK you have and usually very little ground has been lost, if any. It doesn't matter if this error was a year in the making and took you deep into the darkness, the VERY SECOND you turn around, you will begin to see and feel the Light before you again. You may have been going in a loveless direction for a decade, but the very second you pivot around you are already ON the highlighted route and going in the right direction again. Give up hope. You don't need hope. Hope in the journey is a trick of ego used to replace KNOWLEDGE of Principle. Hope is the trick that leads you into hopelessness and disappointment later down the line. What you have is much better and more sure. It is an Internal GPS system which cannot fail no matter how many mistakes you may make along the journey.

So when you make a mistake, turn around as quickly as possible and then make a list of the positive aspects of that very mistake. What have you learned about yourself, the path, forgiveness, and love? Beat the drum of any little bit of good that can be gleaned from it and then let it dissolve back into the nothingness as you gently move forward again with more humility and kindness for yourself and others. All is truly well.

89. Once Again, Cast Your Cares

"Do you really believe you can plan for your safety and joy better than He can? You need be neither careful nor careless; you need merely cast your cares upon Him because He careth for you. You are His care because He loves you." - A Course in Miracles

A S DIFFICULT AS IT MAY BE for you to understand and accept, God is the one Force in the entire Universe which is not ambivalent about you in the least. It is YOU who vacillate in your opinions and feelings about you, your life, your good, and what you want or feel you deserve. And this very ambivalence is what gives rise to your exterior world of praise and blame, loss and gain, bliss and depression. These are all the effects of your own ever-changing sense of self.

In love and perfect gentleness were you created, with a Divine Purpose to love and be loved. This and nothing more is necessary to fulfill your function. Oh my, but you do tend to MAKE things extremely complicated with all your complicated thinking, planning and scheming, resisting, forcing, charging forward and then retreating again. You waste so much time and energy trying harder and harder, when in fact the Answer is to try softer and softer.

You were created by your Creator to create. And as you were created in love and perfect gentleness, so too are you meant to create from love and perfect gentleness. Do you see how opposite this is to the ways of your world? Do you see what it has cost you? And in complete honesty, can you not see how it is NOT working? There is another way.

Soften. Breathe. Let go. And for today, neither advance nor retreat. Simply be still within. Quiet your mind and open your heart to HEAR the still small Voice within with full confidence that you will be answered in the perfect timing in the perfect way. Lean not on your own understanding, but TRUST in That Which is within you, but not of you. Cast your cares on Him for He careth for you. Give all your problems, desires, resistances, dreams and visions to the great Mother Tao and then relax as you walk in Peace and Joy today witnessing the miracles as they gently unfold. You are never "spending" time with Her. You are always "investing" time with the Great Mother for that is where your nourishment comes. Lip service is not enough - invest time with Her today and watch the dividends come in steadily and surely.

Your part is merely to say "yes" when the right opportunities arise, and to say "no" when they are not in alignment with your inner Wisdom. Keep it simple today. Be still, breathe, and listen.

90. Two Worlds

"You see what you expect, and you expect what you invite. Your perception is the result of your invitation, coming to you as you sent for it. Whose manifestations would you see? Of whose presence would you be convinced? For you will believe in what you manifest, and as you look out so will you see in. Two ways of looking at the world are in your mind, and your perception will reflect the guidance you have chosen." - A Course in Miracles

WHO WILL BE YOUR GUIDE TODAY Miracle Worker? Will you consciously choose the One Voice of Infinite Love to guide your day, or will you by default choose the voice which speaks in many contradictory tongues of fear, separation and defensiveness?

The world that you see simply bears witness to the guide that you are choosing in that moment. Looking at the exact same scene, you can see everything quite differently depending on the guide who walks beside you. And these guides are not entities - they are merely thought systems within your own consciousness. There is no volition in them. You are never trapped or stuck except within the story YOU tell yourself. You never lose YOUR free will and the shift in perception can be swift and immediate from one viewpoint to the other as you learn to choose rather than to relinquish your responsibility. Yes, there is freedom, and freedom always brings with it responsibility. It is YOUR responsibility to choose your guide.

The love and peace and joy of God is yours today should you so choose it. There is nothing you need do to earn or deserve it. It IS already within you. YOUR part is merely to activate it by focusing your full attention on it for even a few moments. Whatever you give focused attention to, receives energy and becomes activated by the energy hit. So We suggest that you choose right now - which world would you see today? What are the dominant FEELINGS you want to activate within yourself today? How do you want to FEEL at the end of the day as you close your eyes in bed ready to slumber? What is the energy you want to bring through to YOUR world today?

We are here to Help you. RELAX into the Grace of effortless accomplishment today and release any resistance as you EXPECT and INVITE the world you have chosen. There is no room for hope in any of this. Hope means you have surrendered to the ego's victim consciousness again. Replace all hope with TRUST that in YOUR world, right here, right now, all things are held perfectly in the hands of God. Then, follow your joy and the intuitive hunches knowing that is how We guide you to your ever expanding good.

91. Thought Appears

"The necessary condition for the holy instant does not require that you have no thoughts that are not pure. But it does require that you have none that you would keep." - A Course in Miracles

THOUGHTS COME AND GO LIKE CLOUDS across the sky on a windy day. Many of those thoughts may be fear thoughts, or attack thoughts. The goal is not to rid yourself of all these thoughts but rather to release the tendency you have to hide them in shame or to defend and justify them. There is no need to hide nor to "get rid of" them if you will simply recognize that they are part of the insanity of the ego thought system and that there is no value in them. They are not even YOUR thoughts but rather are the thoughts of a fearful thought system within the illusion. You only really get into trouble when you go about believing these thoughts instead of seeing them for the lies they are.

It is not enough to stop making wrong-minded choices by default. You must practice making right-minded choices deliberately. It is not enough to just stop doing what is destructive, you must also do what is constructive. And this is much easier than you often make it out to be. It is only your resistance which makes it SEEM difficult. In fact, it is EASIER to do it this way.

In other words, it is much easier to dissolve a fear thought of scarcity if you are replacing it with a thought of abundance and plenty. It is easier to calm a child when you are taking away something if you immediately replace it with something else.

The first step is to begin to recognize when you are justifying your attack thoughts with some story - this is quite often a story about how *"they started it."* Perhaps you will begin to see how childish this is and that it is cherished by young and old alike within the ego thought system. If you will now begin to see that it is not making you happy, and if you will see that every ego thought is totally INSANE no matter how justified it is, you may be able to more quickly release any resistance to the process. Honestly ask yourself, *"Would I rather be right, or peaceful?"*

If you can begin to see that any attack thought is insane, you can then also begin to loosen your grip on them. Give them to Us by admitting what they are, and then begin the HEALING by CHOOSING what you want to think instead. Remember, you must always have a POSITIVE clearcut goal for mind to focus on for if you do not, the ego begins to focus on the NEGATIVE goals of what it does not want - and what the ego does not want is peace.

You are a brilliant beautiful Light in an eternal sky. Within you is a Power and a Presence that neither time nor eternity can dull nor diminish. Therefore, there is no reason for you to bow down helplessly before the illusory power of the puny ego thought system. Release insanity and choose peace for you have the ability to do so if you are only willing to deliberately choose the more loving path of sanity and peace today.

92. Choose You This Day

"Decisions are continuous. You do not always know when you are making them. But with a little practice with the ones you recognize, a set begins to form which sees you through the rest." - A Course in Miracles

IF YOU HAVE BEEN MAKING DECISIONS as We've been encouraging you to do, you are by now already feeling and experiencing the outpour of Energy that We've been infusing you with, as well as feeling the gentle Guidance and corrections in keeping you on track. This is a most auspicious time on the Earth plane for anyone who is willing to DO the work necessary to clear out the old lazy sloppy patterns of the past and go for a Life of joyful unfolding.

This is no time to be spiritually passive or immature. Many unforeseen opportunities, promotions and blessings are coming through for those who are BOLDLY stepping up and CHOOSING. Be not afraid of your own power to DECIDE and to CHOOSE dear sisters and brothers. You are not puppets on the string of some etheric Being in the sky. YOU are born Creators and you will either create on purpose, or by default. Pretending that you don't make choices is beneath you and lying to yourself in this way merely wastes your time and life energy. Just look at your own body and you will see the reflection of what you CHOOSE to put in your mouth every day and this should be all the evidence you need to prove that you ARE deciding and that each decision is a cause that creates and effect. You have 100% control over what you eat, and telling the story that you do not only keeps you in a victim role.

It is the same with every area of your life when it comes to YOUR life. We've noticed that those who are not comfortable making their own decisions and goals tend to be

OBSESSED with the decisions and goals of OTHER PEOPLE. Once again, the human problem is not wanting to do YOUR part, but instead wanting to do a part that you CANNOT do - thinking it is unspiritual or too stressful to have a "goal" yourself, but having LOTS of goals for your mate, or child, or co-workers.

STOP trying to control the people around you. Stop judging THEIR choices and decisions. STOP wanting others to make different CHOICES. And all of this will be VERY EASY when you are making YOUR OWN CHOICES FOR YOURSELF. As you grow comfortable in choosing for yourself and in making your own choices, you will begin to release others to make theirs as well, even if they are not the decisions you would choose for them.

Many of you in this Joy Academy are now experiencing the happy demonstrations and synchronistic happenings that are the result of playing with Us in this new phase of your growth and expansion. We are seeding the Earth with tremendous Energies at this time - but We can only do this into the lives of those who are ACTIVELY making decisions and setting goals for themselves. *"Ye have not because ye ask not"* is just as true today as it has been since the very beginning. Fear not, be not afraid. The process is so simple when it comes to deciding. First, go within and center yourself in the Divine Presence. Deeply relax and release all resistance and fear. Breathe and let go. Then, CHOOSE the FEELINGS you want to have concerning the issue or area of life concerned. FOCUS on that feeling and begin to activate it within yourself in the present moment. LET GO of HOW - do not begin to design a plan or strategy - simply marinate in the FEELINGS you want to experience. THEN, see the END result in your Divine Imagination within. BE IN THAT

MOMENT of the end result. Do not linger there - release this Vision to the Presence and Power, and then go about your day and your life, EXPECTING the right doors to open at the right time.

You are Consciously playing with the Power that creates worlds. Have FUN! Enjoy your role and do not get attached to any outcomes. Your particular world can be as full of beauty and Light as you are willing to take out of the Cosmic Art Supply Kit.

93. Better and Better

"I have told you to think how many opportunities you have had to gladden yourself, and how many you have refused. This is the same as telling you that you have refused to heal yourself. The light that belongs to you is the light of joy. Radiance is not associated with sorrow." - A Course in Miracles

LIFE ON PLANET EARTH has never been so wonderful. You are living in most auspicious times in which the Light has never been so radiant and abundant. There is far less struggle, crime, violence, disease, and poverty than ever before and yet now, as in the days of old, when the Light comes the vast majority of humans still prefer the darkness. It is so preferred that it has endless TV channels and news outlets advertising it, even as it wanes. Your social media has been infiltrated by the Chicken Little Syndrome even as your planet continues to evolve and improve. Too bad.

But you are HERE and are reading, which means that you HAVE turned some corner in your Consciousness and are to some degree, large or small, willing and ready to embrace and share the Light of Joy. You ARE choosing to heal yourself bit by bit, by telling a NEW story - a story in which you are no longer focused on healing your "wounds" but have begun to focus on your eternal Wholeness. The Joy Academy is not merely a masthead title affirmation, it is Truth actualized. The Joy is bubbling up and flowing over more and more every week, every day as you all are no longer a vibrational match to the life of passive limitation and active resistance.

Still, do not get sloppy and lazy again. You must remain ever vigilant for the Kingdom of Joy within. Your WORDS are containers for power and are creating YOUR world for you every day. When we hear you year after year telling counselors, *"I suffer from low self-esteem - I'm working on my deservability and worthiness issues,"* We are IMPLORING YOU as We say to you, "THAT IS A TERRIBLE AFFIRMATION - STOP SAYING IT!!! STOP TELLING THAT STORY!" It serves you not. Every perceived limitation that you speak out is creating more of the same in your present and future. And yet, all around you life is thriving and improving and getting better and better. But while you are tuned into the frequency of the old story, you will not hear, see or register the new one. In Consciousness, you cannot watch two different channels at the same time. And again, YOU MUST CHOOSE the channel you want to watch or your subconscious patterns will choose it for you - but YOU ARE ALWAYS THE CHOOSER AND YOU ARE ALWAYS CHOOSING - either consciously and deliberately, or subconsciously by default.

DECIDE now whether you will be joyful today or not. Do not waste a moment "hoping" or wishing for there is not the slightest bit of power there. *"The power of decision is my own"* is more than mere metaphysical posturing. It is TRUTH which must be embraced and embodied in order to be actualized and experienced. Release all cynicism, bitterness and sarcasm today. You are NOT funny in the least and your gallows humor is costing you your HEALTH, WEALTH, PEACE and the loving relationships that would add so much to your joy today and for all eternity. Give up resistance and simply accept the RADIANCE that is your true nature - then, watch while the day brings to you the evidence that life on your planet has never been better or more filled with possibilities for limitless good for you and for all creatures.

94. Love is Love

"There is no difference between love and joy. Therefore, the only possible whole state is the wholly joyous . . .You are being blessed by every beneficent thought of any of your brothers anywhere. You should want to bless them in return, out of gratitude." - A Course in Miracles

THE KINGDOM literally IS the state of joy. To be joyous is to be in the Kingdom. Morose spirituality is excluding the ONE thing that IS Divine. As you have been told, Jesus was frequently misquoted by the Apostles because of their own fearful projections. For instance, He never said "blessed are the poor in spirit for theirs is the kingdom of Heaven." Heaven is a state that IS the ABUNDANCE Principle itself - you cannot get there through an impoverished spirit. It is in fact UNNATURAL to be impoverished for this is a Universe of ABUNDANCE and endless EXPANSION.

Because of these kinds of misguided poverty and sacrifice teachings, the religious world of today is as confused and far from Spirit as were the legalistic Pharisees of Jesus day. Love does not require sacrifice, but it does require making choices. Only ego thinks in terms of sacrifice. It tells you that to choose one thing is to "sacrifice" the other. Spirit sees no such limitation. Renunciation is a favorite ego tactic used to steal your joy - and to steal your joy is another way of saying, to banish you from the Kingdom. The ego loves the concept of sacrifice because it prepares the way for a resentment or grievance later on when you can say, *"But I sacrificed FOR YOU!"*

The many stories of suffering saints is exactly the kind of religious thinking that the ego is so fond of because it excludes any TRULY spirited experience. Remember that you have been told that He need teachers, NOT martyrs. To teach is to demonstrate and as you demonstrate YOUR joy, you teach joy to others. Every joyful thought of anyone blesses all beings who will allow the joy in. Joy increases by sharing it. You cannot become poor enough in spirit to enter the Kingdom but what you can do is surrender your sadness, suffering and pain as simple misperceptions and a misuse of the power of thought.

Mother Theresa is a prime example of one who spoke of service as joy when in fact she was deeply depressed and felt separate from God for decades, all due to misguided religious counseling and thinking. "Service" is another ego concept that actually reinforces separation thinking. Give, feed, and share from JOY, NOT to serve anyone or anything. Do it BECAUSE it feels SO GOOD to do it - because everything you are literally doing to and for yourself - no separation. If you want to serve, serve Principle Itself and in this way you will never have the chance for ego to turn it into a resentment and it will fill YOU up rather than deplete you.

We strongly urge you to turn your thoughts to what you LOVE, for love and joy are the same. Make this a mental habit pattern that carries you through your days. Yes, We are ENCOURAGING you to overuse that word. There are many who say that the word love has been so overused that it no longer has a significant meaning. Again, this is an ego concept. It validates the ego concept of SPECIAL love. Only ego would ever come up with the concept of "too much love" being thrown around. You can love your daughter and love sushi and love rain and love God and love cars - love is love is love is love is love - and all of it joyful when the specialness concept is left behind. The only differences in love have to do with the form that is appropriate as far as expression goes, and any discerning Spiritual Practitioner is spending enough time with Source to be Guided to the proper form for each situation.

We see so much art, so many journals, so much of human expression being of darkness and pain. It is time to turn this around, which is what the word "repent" means - turn around. Begin to bring love to the forefront of your days and watch how the JOY increases. SPEAK MORE of what you love, make daily lists of what you love, start conversations with, *"You know what I love . . . "* Do not make the mistake of becoming poor in spirit for you have the potential to have a spirit of such overflowing abundance that when you walk into any room, the wave of joyous love and delight will be felt like a warm welcoming breeze blowing through as it fills up the hearts of those who do not yet understand that the Kingdom of Heaven is here and now, and that it is a state of Infinite Joy.

95. Come

"Simply do this: Be still, and lay aside all thoughts of what you are and what God is; all concepts you have learned about the world; all images of

everything it thinks is either true or false, or good or bad, of every thought it judges worthy, and all the ideas of which it is ashamed. Hold onto nothing. Do not bring with you one thought the past has taught, nor one belief you ever learned before from anything. Forget this world, forget this course, and come with wholly empty hands unto your God." - A Course in Miracles

CALL OFF YOUR SEARCH and come to the Well of Infinite Goodness and Grace today. Drink deeply from the Living Waters as you release all your thoughts about what you want or need in order to be happy. Release struggle and strain and even release the ideas of winning and losing, loss and gain. Come as a little Child running into the arms of the Beloved Parent.

As you do this, allow your mind to deeply relax - let your thoughts slow down - let go of all worry and strain. Take time to let go of trying to figure everything out - let go of fighting against anything as you rest in the Everlasting Arms, being filled with Light, comfort, healing and direction.

There is a place in you of perfect stillness, perfect calm and serenity. There is a place in you of effortlessness and beauty and Light. It is not a place of laziness or deadness - it is the seat of true Creativity and limitless possibilities for good. It is a place of Alignment. Come to Us. We will meet you there. So much Love awaits you there - and renewal, and rest and more. Delay no longer. Come to the Well with an open heart and mind. Today is your day, this is the time. Leave your story and everything else behind today as you come with empty hands and an open willing heart - ready to be filled and reminded Who you are.

96. You Have What It Takes

"You need a real experience of something else, something more solid and more sure; more worthy of your faith, and really there . . . Say, for example: I am not weak, but strong. I am not helpless, but all-powerful. I am not limited, but unlimited. I am not doubtful, but certain. I am not an illusion, but a reality. I cannot see in darkness, but in light." -A Course in Miracles

YOU ARE NOT YET consistently activating the Power and Truth within you because you still do not consistently remember Who you are. You give in to hope – hope is the opposite of faith and expectancy. As you practice activating your faith and expectancy, you will begin to realize that within you is everything that you need.

"Hoping that it all works out" is a way of saying that you do not expect them to, but that you are still trying to be "positive." This is only slightly better than being all-out pessimistic and negative. It is still a clinging to littleness instead of accepting the Grandeur that is your True Nature. This is the opposite of arrogance because you are claiming a completely impersonal Power that is equally available to all the Children of God. And this is done by the power of the words you speak to yourself. Words are "activators" and should be seen as such.

Positive expectancy activates POWER through faith. This is not an expectancy for specific outcomes – it is not the belief that you will get the "thing" that you want, when you want it, in the way that you want it. This is the expectancy that you have what it takes no matter what is ahead and that you are not alone in the Universe. It is the awareness that all POWER resides in you and that you have the power to magnetize to you all the resources, talent, people, time and energy that you need.

It is the expectancy that even if things work out very differently than you wanted, you will still be able to thrive, prosper and live in peace and joy.

Nothing is too great or too small an instance for you to CONSCIOUSLY use the Power within you because you ARE using it all the time anyhow – it's just that often you are still using it UNCONSCIOUSLY in what you think of as "casual" conversations that go under the heading of "ain't it awful?" This Power is used to invoke parking spaces, or it is used to obscure them from your sight. It is activated to inspire and uplift you, or to terrify and paralyze you. The choice is yours and you choose it through the words you speak verbally and even more so by the words that you entertain in your mind each day.

CHOOSE carefully your words today and AFFIRM frequently: *"I have what it takes to have a wonderful day and I always have what I need!"* And then EXPECT to see a day of evidence that all things are held perfectly in the hands of God.

97. Once Upon a Time . . .

"The body's serial adventures, from the time of birth to dying are the theme of every dream the world has ever had . . . This single lesson does it try to teach again, and still again, and yet once more; that it is cause and not effect. And you are its effect, and cannot be its cause. Thus are you not the dreamer, but the dream. And so you wander idly in and out of places and events that it contrives. That this is all the body does is true, for it is but a figure in a dream. But who reacts to figures in a dream unless he sees them as if they were real? The instant that he sees them as they are they have no more effects on him, because he understands he gave them their effects by causing them and making them seem real." -A Course in Miracles

EAR ONES, you could quite easily start every morning of your life with the phrase, *"Once upon a time . . ."* for each and every day you are telling yourself a story in which the body is the central figure – it is the some "thing" that seems to be acted upon by the other characters within this ongoing script. Of course in Reality, mind is the central figure because mind is writing the script and is the actor, director and even the audience . . . not to mention the critic.

Each moment you are free to tell the story differently. Those of you in New Thought tend to become preoccupied with the writing of the script, but We feel that equally important is the job of the Editor. There are so many moments that you have made into MAJOR scenes which really would have been best left on the cutting room floor if your goal is to be happy and peaceful.

What We are suggesting is this, have at least a weekly Staff Meeting with all the Team Members of mind. In this meeting you can flesh out the general FEELING you want your story to have this week. What are the dominant themes and the tone of the project? Some wonderful themes and tones are: joy, peace, wholeness, success, appreciation and gratitude, unexpected good, love, kindness, prosperity and success, miracles, guidance, effortless accomplishment, radiant health and vitality, cooperation, friendship, laughter and fun, smooth travel, helpfulness, forgiveness, release, acceptance, restoration, romance, affection, new ideas, inspiration, and on and on. Once you've had your weekly meeting, then each morning you can simply re-mind the Mind Team what the focus is, and make sure the Editor is shaping the project into something that is going in the right direction. Remember, the body is not the author of the story – the body is the effect of the story and is to be appreciated and acknowledged for doing such a great job of acting it all out.

If you want the body to change, change the story FIRST. Each and every cell is ready to receive today's instructions. Be clear, gentle and very kind. Now, what is the story you want to tell today?

98. Waiting Patiently

"Those who are certain of the outcome can afford to wait, and wait without anxiety. Patience is natural to the teacher of God. All he sees is certain outcome, at a time perhaps unknown to him as yet, but not in doubt. The time will be as right as is the answer . . . Patience is natural to those who trust. Sure of the ultimate interpretation of all things in time, no outcome already seen or yet to come can cause them fear." - A Course in Miracles

RELAX DEAR ONE, RELAX. Let your thoughts slow down as you breathe in the peace and grace of God. Surrender now your shield and sword of thoughts as you soften into a timeless state of Consciousness. THIS is the way to wait without anxiety and in perfect patience, certain that only good lies before you as you place your past, present and future in the hands of God, knowing that the outcome is certain. To say that the outcome is certain does not mean that a particular form is guaranteed, but rather that when you are in a Consciousness of faith and love, all things work together for good regardless of the form.

Because humans are usually so tied to the illusion of time, waiting is a huge part of the human experience. Most everyone spends a LOT of earth-time waiting. <u>The question is HOW are you going to wait?</u> <u>You are free to make the best of</u>

<u>a waiting period, or you can make the worst of it</u>. You can tell a stressful story to yourself, or a soothing one. You can RESIST the entire time or you can massage your thoughts to better and better-feeling places. This is free will. YOU get to decide HOW you will wait.

And We want to let you in on a little secret, the more resistance you have, the more you slow down the process and prolong your "waiting" experience. This is why "time flies when you're having fun." Without resistance, the experience of being time-bound drops away and moves along quite smoothly.

In fact, the more you practice relaxing all resistance, the more you will release your experience of waiting altogether. It's called "living in the now."

99. *You're Still You*

"Teaching but reinforces what you believe about yourself. Its fundamental purpose is to diminish self-doubt. This does not mean that the self you are trying to protect is real. But it does mean that the self you think is real is what you teach." -A Course in Miracles

TODAY WE WANT YOU TO REACH WITHIN more deeply than usual in order to touch the Eternal Self. This does not require great effort or strain. In fact, it is the absence of effort and strain at last. The daily effort of your world is the clinging to a false self and the endless vain attempts to protect and defend the myth of a weak and separate self, alone in world of bodies.

<u>You are not alone. You are not separate. You are not weak</u>. And nothing that you have ever done – nothing that seems to have been done to you, has changed your essential

REAL Self in the least.

Everyone is teaching every day – and almost continuously. To teach is to demonstrate. You demonstrate not only through your actions, but also through your words. In mind, you narrate your life, giving yourself an interpretation of everything, real or imagined. In this, you are teaching yourself what you think you are. It is what gives you conviction and dissolves "self"-doubt. However, it is often validating the self as alone, insufficient, weak, sinful, damaged, in need, sickly, old, unlovable, failing, broken, and so on. Yet this is exactly the self that should be doubted. It is not real. This is the lesson you must abandon and cease teaching yourself.

To touch the REAL Self begins simply with the recognition that there IS a REAL You already present. Awareness is the first step in healing any mind. There is a real You, in a Real God, and the two are One. Let this nourish and feed you today as you call back your Soul into your awareness. Surrender to this Great Truth today and begin now to teach yourself that this is Who you really are. You really are quite wonderful you know.

Say to your Soul from time to time each day,

> *"Come into my awareness today.*
> *I want to know and feel You in my*
> *life and to demonstrate in simple*
> *ways that there is a Real Me,*
> *living in a Real God,*
> *and the two are One."*

100. Feeling and Form

"What you consider content is not content at all. It is merely form, and nothing else. For you do not respond to what a brother really offers you, but only to the particular ego perception of his offering by which the ego judges it. The ego is incapable of understanding content, and is totally unconcerned with it. To the ego, if the form is acceptable the content must be. Otherwise it will attack the form." -A Course in Miracles

Y OU MUST HAVE NOTICED by now how much of your time and energy is focused on manipulating the forms in your life. And almost every time you are ever upset about anything, it is based on some form that is not to your liking. Then, more energy is used in a mental resistance in which you tell yourself how much happier you would be if current form changed into this, or that, or that, or this.

At this point you may begin getting very busy trying to shift, change and manipulate the form – or you may simply feel powerless and begin spiraling into the various forms of fear: depression, anger, attack, addictive behaviors, and so on.

There is a much better way. We want to speak to you about "*positive manipulation*" as the first step forward in creating miracles. We want you to begin to understand that what is much easier and what brings much faster relief is learning to manipulate the content rather than the form. And the content is the FEELING. And ultimately, this is what you want anyhow. You THINK that the form will automatically bring the feeling/content, but this is just another insane ego fantasy built to keep you dissatisfied.

The non-negotiables in your life should be the feeling/content you want, not the form. Form should be "preferences" rather than demands. For instance, the form of marriage or romantic relationship quite often does not bring the feeling that those who are in it wanted. At the same time, many people who are physically "alone" may feel very connected, loved, and supported. Many very wealthy people "poor mouth" all the time and live in endless financial stress while others with little or no money live in great peace with their needs being met without struggle or suffering. And the opposite of these scenarios can be just as true too.

Now, the way to manipulate feeling is very simple. It is based on the story you tell yourself – it is based on <u>how you perceive the form</u>, not on the form itself. The form is what it is. It is what YOU make of the form that determines how you FEEL – and how you feel IS the content. Right now, you can tell yourself the story of how things are better than they've ever been, and then your mind will build a case to prove this is true by gathering up all the evidence needed. And right now, you can tell yourself it's the worst it's ever been, and mind will begin to gather up the evidence to prove that case.

<u>You are manipulating your feelings all the time without knowing it</u>. You think that feelings just arise out of nowhere and cannot be helped, but this is not so. YOU ARE in charge of your feelings and are actively manipulating them – either deliberately, or by default.

So, how do you want to feel today? What is the content you want to bring forth? DECIDE for yourself, and then tell yourself a story that begins to activate those very feelings. Be kind and patient with yourself. It takes some concentration at first – and WILLINGNESS. For now, let go of the FORM and focus on the FEELINGS you want to have and then start building your case.

101. Go For the Joy

"To be wholehearted you must be happy . . . There is no difference between love and joy. Therefore, the only possible whole state is the wholly joyous."
-A Course in Miracles

PEACE AND JOY ARE THE PRIMARY GOALS of His Course. Forgiveness is merely the path TO the destination – a journey without distance since you are free to experience the goal NOW and in any moment that you choose the peace and joy of God, instead of pain or fear.

In fact, Heaven, God, love and joy are all the same thing. When you are in joy, you are in the kingdom. When you are in joy, you ARE love. When you are in joy, you ARE experiencing God. Simply put, joy is the easiest and fastest path Home. There is nothing to teach but joy. Demonstrate joy and you are automatically leading yourself and others Home. When you see your dog romping through the fields, she is IN the Kingdom – she IS the Kingdom at that moment.

"To become as a child" is to reconnect to your joy. Joy includes giddiness, but is not limited to it. Joy can be very quiet and serene as well. Joy is the open heart and mind. You may experience your internal joy as much at the bedside of dying loved one as at the birth of a child. In joy, the heart, head and gut all come together in cooperation at last.

Joy will lead you to your right life. It is the north-star to your Soul. Find your joy daily and let it guide you.

We leave you with this lesson because We want you to know that His joy IS your greatness and your glory. When we say that you were born for greatness, it simply means you were born from joy, for joy, as joy, to bring joy. What could be more simple and more delightful?

ABOUT THE AUTHOR

Jacob Glass is a spiritual teacher, author, and non-denominational minister. He has been teaching and writing full-time since 1990 throughout Southern California where he resides.

For dates and locations of classes and lectures, resources, inspirational quotes, blogs and information on his CD's and mp3 recordings, please see his website: www.jacobglass.com

32845059R00122

Made in the USA
Middletown, DE
20 June 2016